New Age Strategies To 2X Your Business Cashflow in 6 Months

What Fortune Grade Companies

Will Never Reveal To Small Businesses

JOY GHOSH

Copyright © 2016 GO GETTER STRATEGIES, LLC

WWW.GOGETTERSTRATEGIES.COM

All rights reserved.

ISBN-10: **1536835293**

ISBN-13: **978-1536835298**

DEDICATION

I dedicate this book to my family who inspire and often play hardball with me, encouraging me to go get my dreams and objectives in life.

I also dedicate this book to all the small business owners, entrepreneurs and startups around the world, who live and operate outside the proverbial box, fueled by their high octane creativity, determination, dedication to their cause, courage to persevere despite the odds, to add value to our lives and make our communities a better place to live and play. Kudos to you guys and gals for your contributions. My belief and trust for you is that you always take pride in your battle wounds in this competitive world of new age business – they make you stronger.

TABLE OF CONTENTS

INTRODUCTION 2

1 NEW AGE CASHFLOW ALCHEMY 4

2 TRIBUTE TO THE PAST GENERATIONS 9

3 LEAKY FAUCETS DRAINING YOUR LIFEBLOOD 23

4 BUT SERIOUSLY, THE WOO-HOO STUFF 34

5 INNOVATION OR CONDEMNATION 46

6 READING YOUR ECOSYSTEM'S MINDSET 60

7 RECYCLIC BUSINESS PROCESS RE-ENGINEERING 79

8 MODERN DAY LETHAL KILLER – CYBERCRIME 88

9 YOUR BRAND REPUTATION IS YOUR BOND 97

10 BUSINESS LEVERAGE IN THE NEW AGE 103

11 EARLY RETIREMENT TO YOUR EGO – TODAY 113

12 PROACTIVE TAX PLANNING 122

NEXT STEPS 128

ABOUT THE AUTHOR 132

ACKNOWLEDGEMENTS

I take this opportunity to collectively thank all of my clients across 4 continents over the past 26 years of my career to have so graciously allowed me to serve in their most esteemed organizations. I have learned and expanded my repertoire of skills and capabilities beyond my wildest expectations while I had collaborated with your teams and we collectively worked to create magic in your businesses. It has been an absolute honor and privilege to have served your team to contribute to your success stories. Those life-changing experiences have provided me the audacity and courage to write this book.

INTRODUCTION

ARE YOU SURE THIS BOOK IS FOR YOU? JUST CKECKING ...

I wanted to personally thank you for getting hold of this book. I can promise you that for the right professional and small business owner anywhere in the world, this book will be a goldmine of information that you might not have discovered yet. The world of business is changing at an alarming velocity and it is becoming increasingly challenging for one person to stay intelligently aware of all of it.

However your investment of time and money to get this book will be a total waste and would not add any value at all to your life or business, if you do not meet the basic qualifying criteria. So allow me to list these simple and yet mandatory criteria for you to consider that will enable you to get the most of this book. You must check *all* of them off in order to maximize your investment in this book. If you are not ready to do so yet, set yourself a deadline by when you will be ready to meet these simple criteria to leverage this content in your business.

1. You must be a small business owner, entrepreneur or a startup with at least one year of active participation in

your business.

2. You are willing to think outside the box and beyond the boring textbooks about running a small business.

3. You must be willing to unlearn what no longer serves you and consequently must be willing to learn what does, even if it seems outlandish at first.

4. You must be teachable and concentrate carefully on all the contents of this book, even if some areas seem like a hard punch in the stomach.

5. I am not expecting you to read the entire book in one sitting – I know you don't have the time to do so. However you must be willing to carve out some time in your day to read the book. When you do, please make sure that you are undisturbed and can remember the information you might have read in the earlier pages of the book.

6. Now this is of utmost importance – you must have heard that "Knowledge Is Power". Well that's a lie, since it is only half the truth. "Knowledge is Power *only when you apply it to add value to your life and others*" – that is the complete truth. So, you must be willing to **apply** concepts and steps you learn here in your business – some of them within 7 days of reading that section, without procrastination.

My objective is to get you to a point where you can DOUBLE your business cashflow in SIX months and you have a business to run in parallel. For some of you it could be a stretch goal and for some of you thoroughbreds, "there ain't no mountain high enough". Let's get on with it now, shall we?

1 NEW AGE CASHFLOW ALCHEMY

Cliché as it may sound; **Cashflow is the lifeblood of your business** - period. Sure you have heard that before but how deeply does it resonate with you as a business owner on a daily basis? Does this cashflow thing give you restless and nightmare-filled nights or have you made it your trusted partner and business ally? I have seen wild swings either way in my career. Just like I have witnessed course corrections, I have also witnessed cashflow overflows when the business adopted pragmatic strategies and techniques to keep in tune with the fast changing business dynamics of today.

In today's modern business, cashflow is not a number confined to the scientific calculators and complicated workbooks spanning multiple spreadsheets of the computers of your CPA or the head of your Finance Department. Cashflow has now more than ever, become a TEAM (Together Everyone Achieves More) game. Every department that has anything to do with any financial aspect of your business (can't think of any that isn't) needs to be an integral part of your internal ecosystem that strives for and drives higher cashflow.

You see, by the time the Accountant gets involved to calculate the cashflow of your business, the damage or lack thereof has already been done. While the accountant is responsible for accuracy of the math, the greater accountability and responsibility rests with the other areas of the business that contributed to the components that algebraically add up to result in the net cashflow. Moreover, due to the algebraic nature of the calculation, if one area of the business has taken a hit while another has scored high, the final results may net off just fine from a reporting perspective. This is why cashflow must be considered a TEAM sport rather than an individual play.

Setting aside the Organizational Change Management aspect of this shift, when you or your employees hear this the first time, eyebrows get raised and lips get pursed. Good, if that is how I need to grab your undivided attention, so be it. Why has this shift occurred in modern day business? It's the drive to survive the money crunch, where the speed of innovations in the market drive margins lower and lower, forcing the business to figure out how to make ends meet.

Businesses need to operate lean and mean with the least cost and overheads, with the greatest efficiency, generating the most revenue in the most competitive times in human history. As a business owner in the market today, you are constantly having to juggle these three fundamental parameters to maintain a healthy cashflow pulsing through your business. Take your hawk eyes off just one of this high maintenance trio even for a day and the other two threaten to raise the red alert on your cashflow situation. No rest for the weary these days. But as small business owners, we are humans after all and just like we work smart (not hard), we also need to live and play smart.

How do we maintain that work-life-play balance as small business owners, at times with the most ridiculously limited resources that we have access to? Aha! Welcome to this unique concept of neo-thinking Business Management - I call it **CASHFLOW ALCHEMY**. By the time you are done reading, understanding and more importantly, **applying** what I share with you in this book, you would graduate to the hallowed ranks of cashflow alchemists.

In order to understand what CASHFLOW ALCHEMY is, I encourage you to read the first line of this chapter again. When you are able to maintain a healthy stream of lifeblood through your business, naturally you qualify to enjoy the fruits of that coveted work-life-play balance that small business owners yearn for. As you will learn, when you reduce your operational costs to a bare minimum possible, without compromising on your efficiency and quality and adopt measures to maximize your revenue the three core pillars of cashflow continue to support your business in a strong foundation. Easier said than done, I am sure you will admit but that is exactly what Cashflow Alchemy can do for you.

The purpose of this book is not to belabor upon and repeat the same age-old concepts you learn about cashflow in business school or in your Accounting course, but to share with you some of the most overlooked critical components of your business that affect its lifeblood and hence its solvency. A synergy of the traditional and the new components that you will learn in this book constitutes the new age formula for CASHFLOW ALCHEMY as illustrated in Figure 1.

As the small business owner, a first glance at Figure 1 can give you the jitters – something you might not have anticipated in this new age mumbo-jumbo. It is my job in this book to demystify the puzzle pieces for you to assimilate these new age strategies, share with your team and apply them in your business aggressively to place that 2X in 6 Months objective in your crosshairs.

You will understand each one of these strategies and techniques and how to apply them. I will also indicate as we go along, the timeframe by which you must start to apply them in order to meet your objectives of multiplying your cashflow. The efficacy of this formula lies in the rinse and repeatability of its application so that you can continually achieve higher and higher cash flows in your business. In turn higher cashflow

NEW AGE STRATEGIES TO 2X YOUR BUSINESS CASHLOW IN 6 MONTHS

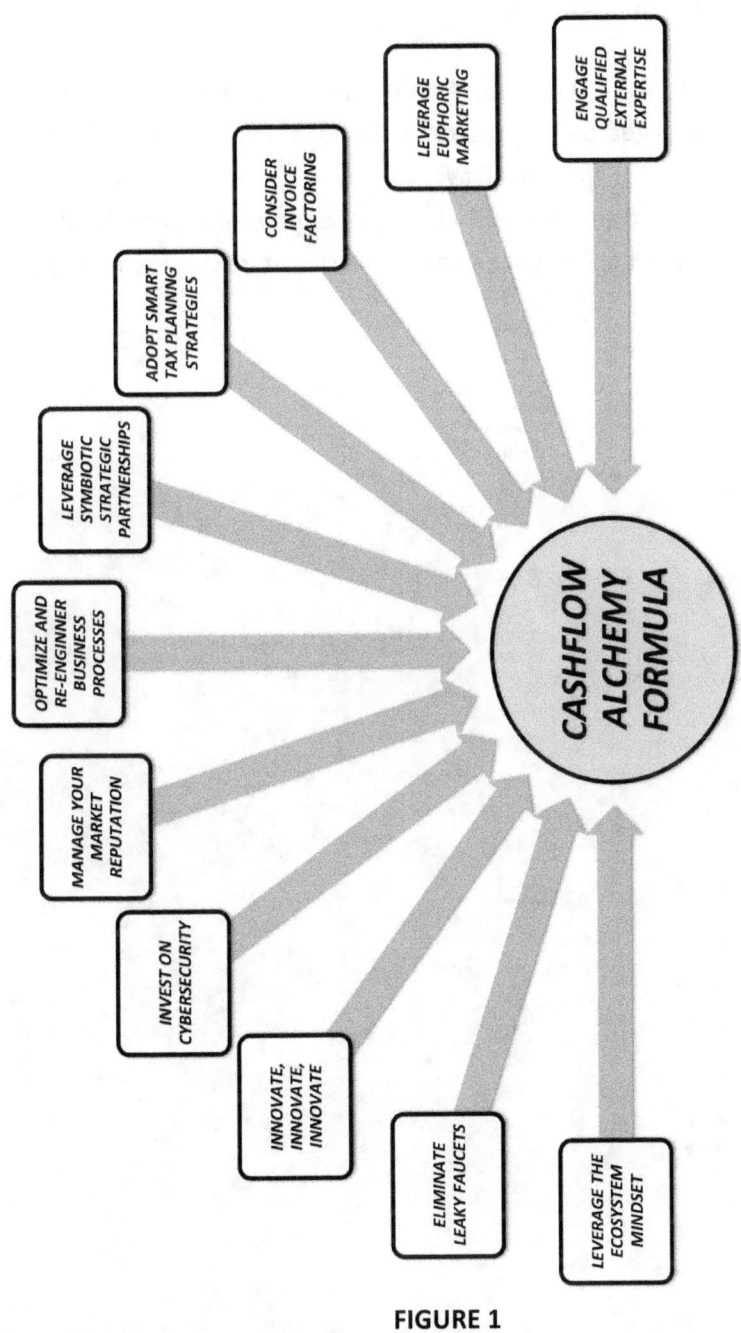

FIGURE 1

would eventually impact your profitability, liquidity, freedom of choice and valuation of your business.

You are about to learn the ingredients of the secret recipe of Cashflow Alchemy, closely guarded by Fortune Grade companies around the world. As the title of this book says, they won't share these with you readily. More importantly you now have the opportunity to apply what you learn from this book in your small business and master the new age cashflow game.

Let's roll ....

2 TRIBUTE TO THE PAST GENERATIONS

For the purposes of posterity, the traditional rules of managing cashflow are still valid. For the completeness of this book, we need to make due diligence with a quick recollection. As a small business owner, who may very well be wearing multiple hats at the same time, we must not overlook the time-tested fundamentals of cashflow management.

Here's the fundamental formula for cashflow calculations that hold true even in this new age of business

FIGURE 2

Pretty straightforward, huh? Net business liquidity is what keeps the lights on in your business, while the net business liability is what depletes those hard-earned funds that keep those lights on in your business. The difference between the two as in Figure 2 determines your net business cashflow. However that's just what shows above the

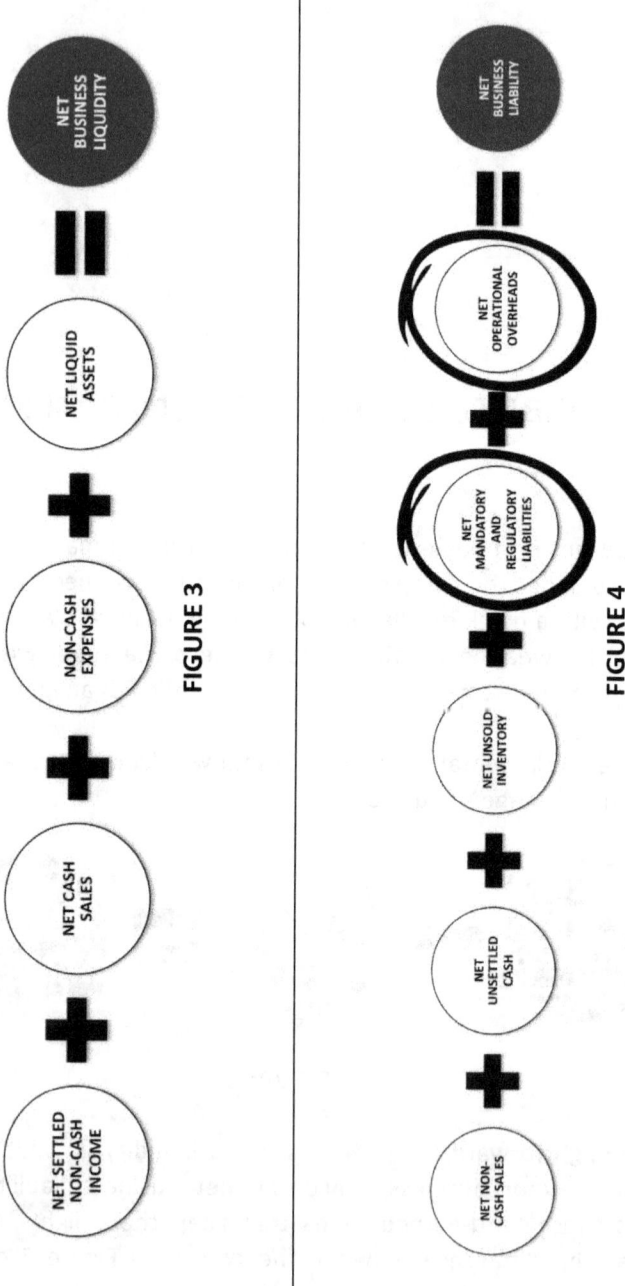

FIGURE 3

FIGURE 4

waterline. The real iceberg lurks deeper below as illustrated in Figure 4. Let's break down each component of both the liquidity and liability buckets for a better understanding of how the new age strategies that you are about to learn can have an impact on the net business cashflow.

First of all let's consider the Liquidity Factors from Figure 3.

NET SETTLED NONCASH INCOME : These would be all your cleared receivables from open invoices, cashed checks, money orders from customers, EFTs, money transfers and credit card settlements after any chargebacks and refunds. Essentially all the hard currency that shows in your bank account would come in this category.

NET CASH SALES : These would be any over the counter hard currency that you received from customers who purchased directly from your store or office location, but have not yet been deposited in your bank account.

NON-CASH EXPENSES : These are checks that you wrote out to your vendors or other deferred payment methods you used to clear your payables and liabilities, that have not been cashed yet, so the money is still in your bank account right now – the debit had not occurred yet.

NET LIQUID ASSETS : Some Accountants would frown to include these to be part of cashflow, but I like to count them in due to their liquidity despite some possible depreciation. These are essentially any assets that could be liquidated right away for cash without any penalty or levy whatsoever, if you had to. Examples could be paid off vehicles, watercraft or other equipment your business owns, that a ready-to-purchase buyer would take off your hands in exchange of its FMV (fair market value) or other negotiated price. Paid off real property owned by the business may come up for consideration as a liquid asset – I would rather defer to your accountant based on the prevailing laws in your jurisdiction, to give guidance on this one.

Now let's consider Figure 4 and analyze the Liability Factors of your business. This where it starts to get a little more complicated and this is where some of the new age business dynamics come into place to impact the two factors circled in Figure 4. Hang in there with me and I will walk you through them shortly.

NET NONCASH SALES

THE LIABILITY: These are all the sales of your products and services you have made and agreed to accept non-cash payment methods such as checks, money orders, credit cards. These are deferred payment methods and there is a risk that you may not be able to collect the money after all. Checks may bounce or take longer to arrive, or arrive with less amount than what was invoiced. Credit card payments may be fraudulent purchases or the customer may initiate a chargeback. Money orders may get delayed in the mail, if not get eaten by the dog, or sent to the wrong address. These are liabilities for your business until the cash is in the bank.

THE MITIGATION: Online payments have gained popularity due to the timeliness and accuracy at which money hits your bank account. The pre-authorization process built into online payment processing systems ensure that a payment does not bounce like a check would. For large ticket items, a credit card may not be feasible to use due to the high processing fees, which can definitely be considered operating expense for tax deduction purposes. But they are still considered a liability for the cashflow equation. Electronic checks, bank transfers, EFT or even the increasingly popular online currencies like Bitcoin may be better suited for your business for shorter lead times to encashment and greater assurance of payment for larger ticket items.

NET UNSETTLED CASH

THE LIABILITY : Top off those non-cash sales with deferred payment terms that you might have agreed upon with your customer. Is the payment due immediately on delivery or can the customer enjoy the product or service for free for 15 or 30 or 45 days before they are required to pay for it? In the interim, you don't have the money in your bank and hence is a liability for your business.

Some service oriented businesses with subscription plans would bill and get paid at the beginning of the billing period but according to GAAP (Generally Acceptable Accounting Principles) that are followed all over the world, this revenue cannot be classified as earned revenue until the end of the billing period until the services are considered 'delivered'. So even if you have the cash upfront, you cannot technically consider that yours until the end of the billing period. The customer could cancel their subscription and ask for a refund. So, the money that you might have collected is not yours – yet. If you have gone past the billing period, then you have a rightful claim to that cash that had already been deposited in the bank. Then it flips over to the Liquidity portion of the cashflow equation in the new period. But in the current period, such subscription payments need to be considered in your Liability section.

Another real life example that comes to mind is product trials or even companies that offer a 15 - 30 day money back guarantee. You as a business owner are allowing the customer to use the product on a free trial basis and may be charging a modest amount or nothing at all to allow the customer to test the waters. You have agreed with the customer to automatically bill them or charge them if they don't call in to cancel the order before the trial period expires. Well the customer forgets all about the trial period and you charge their card or send them a bill to pay with the expectation that they will honor that request. If they do, you're golden and money is moving from a liability to liquidity. However if they don't, they ask for a refund by cancelling the order or even bypass you completely and initiate a chargeback with their bank.

This is not a good situation to be but that is the cost of doing business. At the end of the day, unless the payment comes in after the trial is over, it is a liability for your business. In case of a chargeback, it is actually even worse, since the bank would penalize you with a fee for the chargeback that hits you directly as a liability.

Most definitely this is a problem with product trials and its impact on your cashflow. I will address this issue with some mitigation strategies later on in this book. In some countries this concept of a money back guarantee does not exist – you buy it and it's yours to keep whether you like it or not. I won't debate on the business ethics involved in this practice but there are several consumer behavior and demographic factors to consider here, which prompts businesses to adopt such a stance with their customers.

Essentially these are all the stuck up money or unsettled cash as open receivables or deferred revenue, although you might have already delivered the product or service. The uncertainty of these transactions makes it part of the liability portion of your cashflow equation.

THE MITIGATION : The mechanics of doing business does not allow for a universal guideline to use the short lead-time payment methods to be used all the time. While working with large corporations and government agencies, as a small business you don't have much choice other than to offer payment terms. This is sometimes considered a factor for the bidding process. One strategy to use that has proven effective in my experience is to use a tiered payment term.

Essentially you are saying *"Ok Customer, if you pay me within 7 days of this invoice date, I will give you a 10% discount. Pay me within 15 days and I will give you a 5% discount, or you can pay me in 30 days on actuals."* So you see, there is an incentive for the customer to clear their payable quickly, since that would potentially help them with a lesser payment for the same product or service. In addition to the above, consider including an additional clause, *"We reserve the right to levy an interest of up to 10% APR on payments cleared after 30 days."* Whether you will exercise that right or not in case of delayed payments is entirely up to you, but it gives you legal leverage in the purchase contract to do so if needed. At the same time, the client is watchful about their payment schedules so that they don't create a reason for you to exercise that right.

Having said that, depending on how big your small business is, the nature of relationship you have with the client, the criticality, or for that matter the indispensability of your products and services in their business operations, you would want to use your discretion on asking for such terms of payment.

For subscription-based businesses where you are unable to claim ownership of the cash even if you have received it upfront, there isn't much you can do from an accounting practice perspective. Just ensure that you continue to deliver whatever you agreed to do, so that the client continues to stay satisfied and use your products or services without any mid-term cancellation. You may include in your contract that mid-period cancellations will not be eligible for a refund and that you need a 30-day notice in writing if the customer wants to cancel. That way you can be assured of the cash coming in with you being able to predictably consider the inbound cash as an asset.

Product trials and period-bound money back guarantees are not handled properly from a liability risk mitigation perspective in my opinion. Even large corporations don't do it right. Consider sending a reminder to the client 3-4 days before the expiry of the trial or money back guarantee period as a courtesy customer satisfaction call. You are actually speaking to the customer on the phone or in person or even using text messaging. Emails are not effective here because not every one checks their emails on time and for all you know they may have a spam filter that blocks it out completely. The idea behind this courtesy call to not only to show your support and their opinion, but also to be a reminder that the trial or money back guarantee period is coming up. If the customer would not be keeping your product or service then you can address the problem right away and take care of the refund or the cancellation of the order at no charge. This is far better from a cashflow perspective. Why? Because if you did not know the customer's intent on time and no refunds are allowed after say 14 or 30 days, the customer may still reach out to their bank and attempt a chargeback against you. If the bank honors that chargeback then they impose a fee on you – not on the customer.

NET UNSOLD INVENTORY

THE LIABILITY : If you are selling physical products and are stocking up on these products in a warehouse that you own, they contribute to the stuck up hard cash that you are carrying in your business. Consider the additional overheads of the real estate, the utilities involved in that warehouse, the payroll costs for staff managing that warehouse, the insurance premiums for that warehouse, the security and other technology you have in place to operate that warehouse. Collectively, all of these costs are locked up unless a product is sold at a profit, to offset some of these overheads including the cost of the product.

If you are running a consulting company with consultants in your payroll, every hour that your consultants are not exchanging their time for money, is considered unsold inventory for your company. In this case, any "utilization" below 100% is considered unsold inventory. Your consulting business is essentially carrying the prorated compensation package of the unutilized or under-utilized employees. It is also carrying your traditional regulatory liabilities of having employees as a direct cost, without being offset in exchange of their time for money from a client. If however the consulting company used contractors paid by the hour, there is no "unsold" inventory per se for the company itself, since there is usually no cost incurred for the hours for which the contractor was not engaged in a client billable activity.

Similarly, if you are a repair and maintenance company and your revenue comes from the number of hours your technicians actually performed their service in exchange for the fees, you also have to deal with unsold inventory. Like the consulting company, your unsold inventory would be the number of hours your service technicians did not get the opportunity to provide service in exchange of the service fees from an end client.

THE MITIGATION : Demand Forecasting (DF) and Demand Planning (DP) is as much an art as it is a science and when you master that, "unsold" inventory ceases to cause heartburn or reduces that burn whether you are a product manufacturer or a service provider. Truth be told, regardless of size, businesses have varying degrees of competency on DF and DP and when this is not done right, unsold inventory can be quite a big hole in your cashflow.

If you are a manufacturer, just-in-time manufacturing is a widely used practice if you do it right and have a reliable supply chain in place. If you don't then you would tend to manufacture a little more than the demand. After all you would rather manufacture a little extra than tell a ready to buy customer that there is a lead-time before they can get your product. But then you need to factor in the costs of holding that extra inventory in house, inventory that may never get on a delivery truck.

If you are in that situation, you may want to consider contract manufacturing where it is your design, your suppliers, your intellectual property, your patent protected product, but you have outsourced the manufacturing to another company. They take care of the production, place your label on the product and it is ready for you to pick up and send to your customer. Most definitely they would make sure that they don't overproduce or else they would stay stuck with your items. Some of these contract manufacturers would also hold the inventory in their warehouse for a fee.

Alternatively you could have another company hold your inventory as consignment stock. You own the inventory, but don't have to carry the overheads of having the infrastructure to hold that inventory. When an order comes you send the order to that company and they take care of the shipping, returns and payment processing. A highly viable and successful model in this regard is FBA (Fulfillment By Amazon), which has come in as an absolute long-awaited boon for small manufacturers and distributors. Today, FBA is changing lives of millions of small business owners.

If you are in consulting or provide a service, you still need to perform DF and DP – no way around that. You must proactively manage your workforce with the objective of keeping everyone exchanging hours for dollars. Easier said than done of course but that's where the rub is. Picking up long term contracts with a well negotiated scope and room for additional change orders are ideal for such companies. This allows them to hire employees with a decent runway to keep them utilized 100% of the time. Ensure that you are evaluating customer feedback and performing regular performance reviews of your employees to ensure that you retain those who score high and figure out a way to re-tool, retrain or retire those who don't meet the standards. While it would be easy to engage the high performers in subsequent projects, resources with inadequate skills, despite their low cost of service could be a risk from an unsatisfied customer.

For short-term contracts, look into your under-utilized or un-utilized resources, compare their skillset and get them engaged. If this is not possible, consider hiring competent contractors on a time bound contract with decent margins for your revenue numbers. You don't own that Intellectual Capital of this contractor for sure, although you or your client would own the Intellectual Property that these contractors create in the project. However this ensures that you don't have to deal with unsold inventory.

NET MANDATORY AND REGULATORY LIABILITIES

THE LIABILITY: These are all your mandatory expenses – salaries and wages, employee benefits, payments made in cash to vendors, payables due to government or regulatory agencies, fines, penalties, compulsory certifications and training, lawsuits as a petitioner or respondent requiring you to pay legal fees.

While some of the above categories are obvious and have not changed for centuries, some of these have expanded in scope and severity in the new age of business. I have dedicated Chapter 8 of this book to precisely address these new age threats and dynamics of doing business that a lot of small business owners don't understand or pay much attention to. Flying under the radar or looking the other way, just because you have a small operation does not work anymore, as I will explain in the forthcoming chapters.

THE MITIGATION: Due to the breadth of the scope of such mandatory liabilities that reduce your cashflow, it would be more prudent to address these in the forthcoming chapters as I take you through these different new age business dynamics.

However for the purpose of summary, adopting measures that will help you keep your distance from the law and the courthouse needs to be first and foremost in your mind. This applies to your practices for

- paying sales and income taxes accurately and on time,
- staying compliant with the stated regulations in your industry,
- ensuring that your products don't end up being a plausible cause for threatening or harming life and property,
- securing the confidentiality of the PII (personally identifiable information) or NPI (non-public information) of your clients,
- enforcing clear, consequential and stringent HR policies in your employee handbook for employee conduct
- paying your vendors on time with well maintained records

We will cover some of these in the forthcoming chapters of this book.

NET OPERATIONAL OVERHEADS

THE LIABILITY: These are all your operational overheads that I have not talked about so far – business and travel expenses that you pay to a vendor or reimburse to your employees, employee training, lease payments, rents, insurance premiums, payments to contractor and service providers, communications, loan payments, corporate credit card payments, utilities, rents, cleaning and janitorial services, shipping costs, – I am sure you will add more to the list for your business.

Gosh, as a business owner I sometimes wonder how we make any money to run our business and our lives, after paying all these liabilities. I guess that's where the fun is – out of nothing, we small business owners create magic – won't you agree?

THE MITIGATION : It all boils down to an ROO (Return On Overheads) analysis that you must do at least every month-end to accurately know and decide if there is an overhead you could cut out without impacting the efficiencies of your business operations? Some of these overheads are a "must-have" there's no way around that and you can't eliminate them. But can you reduce the amount you are paying on a monthly basis in order to throttle the outflow of cash? Could you renegotiate that lease or that rent? If you are owning real property for your business would it make sense just to sell and rent out commercial space? 'No' is an easy answer and probably an escape route to be blunt about it. Sometimes it's our ego that gets in the way. Look what's more important? Your ego or a higher cashflow in your business?

Do you really need that much insurance for your business? Could a model such as FBA (Fulfillment by Amazon) or other consignment stock and third party drop shipping leave more cash in your bank at the end of the day? Could you cut down on staff travel with better technology and remote services ? Could you renegotiate more favorable terms with your employee benefit providers ? Do you really need to leave all the electrical equipment, lights, fans, air-conditioners on after hours?

These are nothing new to you and as a small business owner you may already be doing some or all or even more of these overhead slashing measures right now. What else could you do? If you are out of ideas, maybe talking to an external expert can help.

Overhead reduction is an ongoing improvement process – a journey, definitely not a destination. Every business is different, making the appropriate measures also different.

As you can understand from this Chapter, cashflow changes from day to day. As a business owner your objective is to reduce your liability and increase your liquidity in order to enjoy a healthy cashflow pulsing through your business month after month.

3 LEAKY FAUCETS DRAINING YOUR LIFEBLOOD

One of my biggest lessons learned during my long inter-continental tenure working with Fortune grade companies and Fortune grade wannabe companies, was to identify the so-called "leaky faucets" that commonly get overlooked during the regular course of business. Once they are identified, counter-measures become necessary to plug these leaks and stop the drainage. Some of these trolls in your cashflow though negligible when considered on an individual transaction basis, can assume gigantic proportions over time and frequency.

While major corporations have the stomach to take a few blows before someone takes notice and corrective action, small business owners often don't have the luxury of a buffer to sustain such an atrophy of business cashflow. So in this chapter, let's look at some of these trolls that may be strolling un-noticed in your business and increasing your liability portion of the cashflow equation. Once we find them, we'll discuss how you can take them out of your business.

However, for the completeness of this Chapter let's understand a few basics about Cashflow Management. What is your motivation to do anything different than what you may already be doing in your business right now, to show better figures on your cashflow calculations? As a small business owner, depending on your area of primary focus on your business, Cashflow Management may very well be a headache you don't want to bear. Quite candidly, that's a risk in itself for your business.

WHY IS CASHFLOW IMPORTANT FOR ANY BUSINESS

Now that you understand the basic formula and concept of CASHFLOW MANAGEMENT, let's get into a discussion on why it is important for every business regardless of size, to blink one eye at a time when it comes to paying close attention to the lifeblood of the company.

Traditional accounting systems do not calculate cashflow and they are more geared to profit and loss calculations. A surprisingly large number of business owners think of the profit (or loss) as their cashflow, which is an incorrect interpretation.

Going back to the CASHFLOW formula in Figures 2, 3, and 4, as a business owner, you must be well aware of each and every component of liquidity and liability in your business. That is what you need to measure, monitor, adjust, eliminate and repeat the process over and over again with the objective of increasing your cashflow. How do you increase cashflow? Mathematically simple from Figure 2 – increase liquidity AND reduce liability. In real life, the closer you can get to this two-pronged approach working simultaneously in your business, the more ideal it would be to stretch the difference and hence maximize your cashflow.

So why is cashflow so important to any business?

It's FREEDOM to MAKE CHOICES in your business that become possible when you have a pile of cash waiting to be tapped into. The more liquid cash you have in hand to leverage in your business, higher the flexibility you have to operate your business. Here are some of the benefits:

- Investment decisions that would add value to your business are easier to make.

- Loans may not be necessary to run your business if you have large liquidity, thereby relieving you from the liability of those high interest payments and pesky creditors.

- Hiring of qualified talent, expansion of your business operations for greater coverage of your footprint in the market are all possible if you have higher cashflow in your business.

- Need to purchase some capital equipment? No problem if you have cash on hand to pay for it upfront in full. You get to purchase at the lowest possible price without the need for financing. This also helps you in maximizing the NAV (net asset value) of your capital equipment so that you can calculate the depreciation of the asset for tax purposes based on the maximum NAV as opposed to a complicated calculation of the depreciation based on the amount you actually paid and the amount that is still under financing.

- Need to spend a few extra dollars on marketing to inject some additional sales in your business? With higher cashflow, you have the freedom to do so.

- Need to expand into newer markets to open newer doors for your business? Well with cash in your hand, you can absolutely do that.

- Looking for a corporate investor or VC firm to infuse some funds in your business? Or perhaps you are looking for a buyer. Cashflow rich companies, especially private companies are very exciting for such investors and buyers, due to the lower risk to their investment or purchase decision.

Why don't you make a list of all that you wanted to do with your business but had no choice but to hold back because you did not have access to liquid cash in your business? With access to a positive and healthy cashflow, maybe it is time to revisit that list and do some cherry picking once again and make that wish come true after all.

Generally speaking, the cashflow calculation must be diligently done as part of your month-end closing process, so that you can get a good handle of your cashflow situation at the beginning of the new month, allowing you to take corrective action as necessary during the month to get better numbers next month.

I know some business owners who micromanage their cashflow with weekly or even daily calculations. Whether such micromanagement is necessary is a matter of debate and conjecture and personal preference for sure. However such micro-management is more a sign of uncertainty and unpredictability in the business than any real merit to such intense monitoring. Cashflow can be a Titanic for some businesses and results take months to show after corrective action is consistently taken.

A month is typically a good time period to calculate cashflow, make comparisons with past performances and make forecasts for the future months. A month-long monitoring period provides ample time for non-cash transactions to settle - both from a receivables and payables perspective to provide a more accurate picture of the true cashflow situation of the business. Any monitoring period lesser than a month is generally regarded as an overkill and could actually be misleading. Such micro-management may prompt knee-jerk reactions and potentially hasty decisions, which may damage the business more than what those reactions were intended to correct.

A steady cashflow that rises or at least flatlines in the positive for a few months can provide a lot of flexibility for making business decisions. It can even grant you with the courage to take some calculated risks to expand your operations and increase your cashflow. This flexibility and freedom would generally not be possible if your cashflow graph is sliding down and you are always wearing that dreaded fire fighting hat in your business.

Can a healthy operating cashflow for your business create a competitive advantage in your favor? Absolutely and you can bet a dollar to a donut that the most formidable competitor in your market is already winning the game of a healthy cashflow in their business, which is probably why they are leading the pack on your turf.

Think objectively about where your business is right now, where it ranks in your market let's say by way of market share. I know this could come as a hard blow in the gut but take one for your team and make an honest assessment of your current market share. Now, what is the market share of the company that is leading the pack? If those numbers are not in public records and without taking the risk of corporate espionage, make an honest estimate of what that market share could be? I know it's hard to give credit to the competition, but that assessment is actually a goldmine that might have remained hidden from your line of sight.

A deeper root-cause analysis of the difference in the numbers would most likely be attributed to the cashflow between their business and yours. The freedom of greater cashflow allows the flexibility for more innovation, investment in higher quality of products and services, expansion into more geographic locations, the ability to attract better quality talent with higher compensation, more incentives for employees, customers and investors, more marketing muscle across different channels where the customer base is hanging out. All of these collectively contribute to a larger footprint in the market for the business with a higher value proposition than yours.

If your business is the leader in the pack then you are already in the zone and have mastered the magic of a healthy cashflow. You also know that the rest of the pack is doing everything they can to follow your footsteps to win the cashflow game. So what do you do? A master never reaches the end - a master always creates the perceived end... and that is exactly what you would do if you are leading the pack in your industry. You leverage your cashflow to create new frontiers to push the limits further and further and keep leading the pack, retaining your competitive advantage in the market and widening the gap.

So where is your business right now and where does it need to be in a year or 5 years from now - not in your egoistic opinion, but in your unbiased vision? Cashflow is the lifeblood of your business. The question is - are you feeding it with refreshing oxygen or are you suffocating it with noxious agents? We have covered some of these noxious agents that add to your liability. Let's dig a little further to find some additional leaky faucets in your small business that is eroding your cashflow numbers silently. When we find them let's plug them once and for all.

CAN PINCHING FOR "PENNIES" HELP YOUR CASHFLOW ?

Oh yes, and I encourage you not to take this lightly because if you have pinched 100 pennies, you would have made a dollar right into your bottom-line and into your cashflow. Whether you want to pinch for pennies or not is a personal preference and also your style of running your business. It may be a matter of ego for you to even read what I am about to suggest - let alone apply them. It may seem ridiculous or "beneath your pride" to even consider some of these options. But hang with me here for a while and you will hopefully understand how a penny saved can really be a penny earned and 100 of those puts that dollar right back into your cashflow.

BUSINESS LOANS: In the competitive business finance market today, have your looked at the interest rates on your business loans? When was the last time you did a market research on other lending options that are available with lower interest rates and terms? Financial institutions are fighting for customers and even a 10th of a percentage can bring you significant savings that goes right into your cashflow. Shop around and if required, play a little hardball with your lender when you find a better rate elsewhere. Everyone hates to lose business. Whenever you sign loans always make sure that there is never a pre-payment penalty involved. This gives you the flexibility to refinance and move on to a better rate. I recommend you do this exercise every 6 months to ensure you are still getting the best lending rates you could get in the market.

BUSINESS CREDIT CARDS: Similar to business loans, you may want to consider performing a market research every quarter to 6 months to find cards that have lower interest rates than the one you have. If you and your employees carrying those cards are not paying the balance off in full every month, then you may be paying some pretty hefty interests on them when you cumulatively calculate everyone's carry over balances. Whenever possible choose business cards that gives your business rewards points for every dollar your spend. For corporate cards, the membership reward points are for your business and not for your employees who carry then. Those points may be exchanged for small to medium purchases to pay for some of your business expenses including business related travel.

BANK ACCOUNTS: All banks are not created equal - yes even they have cutthroat competition between themselves. Perform at least an annual audit to determine if another bank would offer you more interest on your balances and/ or not charge those fees for banking services that you may be currently paying. If you do, consider changing banks or even check if your current bank can match or improve on those numbers to keep your account with them.

SLOW MOVING OR OBSOLETE INVENTORY: If you are into Manufacturing, Repair or Logistics, and maintaining warehouse space you are paying quite a large amount of money on insurance premiums and other overheads that we have already spoken about. When was the last time you ran an "ABC" report of your inventory? Take a hard look at those "C" inventory items and even some "B" items. If they are slow moving, well it might be better to just sell them off at a huge discount or barely above cost so that you can stop paying premiums for them.

Alternatively think about bundling them with other faster moving items as limited time bonuses to clear the inventory balance. If there are items that have not moved for the last 3-6 months depending on your typical lead-time to sell, see if you can salvage and repurpose the components. Would those items be something a Thrift Store can pick up and move them for you? Can't hurt to check that possibility.

I have seen some of my clients move such B and C category items to other markets – even as an export to another country in an effort to move them from the on-hold inventory. As a small business, you may not be in the export business, but could you strike up a relationship with another business cross-border who might be interested in such products and pick them off your hands to sell in their market?

Otherwise it may make more sense to just dump them at cost or just take a write-off. Such measures not only reduce your insurance premiums and other overheads but may also provide your business a tax advantage.

MEMBERSHIP REWARDS – Pick them up everywhere as much as possible for your business purchases. If there is a coupon or discount available because you are a member, take advantage of them for business purchases. You will be surprised how much these add up into your cashflow at the end of the year.

Now let's flip the coin on Membership Rewards for your business. Do you have a Loyalty Program for your business? If not, why not, especially if you have the potential for repeat customers? Several online Loyalty Programs are available in the market that work entirely through simple scans of QR or barcodes at the point of sale. If the online programs don't work for you to integrate with your purchasing process, well, build one for yourself that suits your specific needs. These online programs have been designed not only for customer acquisition, but also for customer retention and repeat business with the same customer - all of which brings in more revenue with least overhead.

DEALS IN THE MARKET– Look for them everywhere not just in your favorite store that you visit for personal items. Several online comparison-shopping sites are available for you to find the best deals in the market. Have you considered Amazon or eBay for the next item that you need to purchase for your business. If not, why not? You may be pleasantly surprised at the prices you can get from these behemoths in the e-commerce industry.

Have you considered picking up a membership of Amazon Prime if you are a frequent business shopper at Amazon? Free shipping and priority shipping is waiting for your business for your purchases with your

Amazon Prime membership. So unless you are in the market for the new Cessna or a Lamborghini or a private yacht or for that matter the next rocketship to Mars, do check out Amazon for your next business purchase – you may be pleasantly surprised.

TAX DEDUCTIBLE DONATIONS : Do you have old computers, higher mileage vehicles, other electronic equipment or furniture that are no longer good enough for your business? Instead of recycling or sending them to the garbage dump, them, why not consider donating them to non-profit organizations for a tax deduction? Depending on what you have to give away, this may save quite a few dollars in corporate taxes.

HYBRID / ELECTRIC VEHICLES IN YOUR FLEET: If your staff operates a fleet of gasoline or diesel powered vehicles for your regular operations, consider transitioning into hybrid or electric vehicles. This way you not only reduce your carbon footprint to help the environment, you can get at least 3-5 times better mileage using such vehicles reducing your fuel expenses. This would make a huge positive impact on your cashflow situation and make you feel good of having made your contribution for the environment as well.

SWITCHING TO SOLAR POWER: Depending on your location and the type of brick and mortar infrastructure you have for your business operations, consider the ROI of switching to solar power instead of the traditional electrical grid. If you own the real estate for your business this is easier to decide. If you are leasing your space, it can't hurt to speak to your landlord about installing solar power in the building. Alternatively, look for similar workspace where the facilities are powered by solar and consider relocation.

For sure there is upfront cost to do the installation so you need to work with the solar company and your Executive Leadership Team to consider and calculate the time it will take for you to recover the costs. Depending on the type of deal you strike with your solar panel installation company, you could consider the amount you pay as Op-Ex (operating expense) instead of Cap-Ex (capital expense) from a tax perspective. Either way you save money on taxes as you continue to slash those energy bills for your business.

STRICT ENERGY POLICY : This brings us to a good lead into structuring a strict energy usage policy for your business, whether you are able to switch to solar or not. I would even go as far as placing this in your Employee Handbook to make sure that your employees are aware of this energy policy for the business.

Essentially this corporate policy defines how energy should be used in your business. Lights and other electrical equipment without exception (and within reason) need to be powered down if they won't be utilized after hours or even during regular hours. Traditional fluorescent or incandescent lights need to be replaced with LED technology. Air-conditioners and other heavy equipment need to be used on an as needed basis. The same power-down policy must absolutely apply to such equipment. Every bit helps the grid and puts dollars right back in to your business cashflow.

If you have a fleet of vehicles to operate your business, we talked about switching to hybrid/electric vehicles. In addition, operators need to use modern GPS technologies like Google Maps or even Wayz to find the shortest route from point to point considering the most current traffic conditions to save on fuel costs and reduce your carbon footprint.

You get the point here I am sure. As small business owners we tend to overlook the obvious because we are so busy doing what we do best – serve our customers and make money. So what trolls are strolling in your business to erode your bottom-line? Seek and terminate a.s.a.p.

4 BUT SERIOUSLY, THE WOO-HOO STUFF

CAUTION : SKIMP ON THIS AND EVERYTHING ELSE YOU DO IS USELESS.

I promised you to reveal some really cool new age stuff in modern day business and this is a Chapter you are not taught in Business School and most definitely not part of any exam that you might have taken in the world of business. Granted I have written two Amazon bestsellers on Self-Development. I kid you not, if you master what you are about to learn in this Chapter, the price you paid for this book and/or the time you invest to read it will be worth many more times over. This is the fundamental core foundation of your life and of your business, so place close attention and perhaps you would want to read this Chapter again just to seal it in. This is not some Woo-Hoo stuff, it is not pep talk or some inspirational mumbo-jumbo. It's pure neuro-science and the truth behind how we humans are wired to operate to create our reality.

You are not in business for the money. You are not in business because you want to be your own boss. You are not in business because you don't want a 9-5 routine driven grind for an employer. You are absolutely not in business because you want to prove to the world that you are a big shot with the big mansion, the fancy car or that private jet.

Shocked? *"What on earth are you talking about, dude?"* Yup, I said it. Calm down, take a few deep breaths and I encourage you to dig deep inside to find the truthful answer to my question, *"Why are you in business?"* Perhaps it will help by cutting out all the noise outside and closing your eyes for a moment of self-reflection.

Let's understand how you and me and everyone else who you deal with in any part of your life is wired to operate in life and in business. Therein you will find one of the most closely guarded secrets of successful companies around the world and all the wonder kids who continue to surprise us so-called veterans of the last generation.

You may not care about the human anatomy, I am not a medical doctor and this is not a lesson on brain surgery. However that does not imply that we can ignore the mechanics of what makes us function as people.

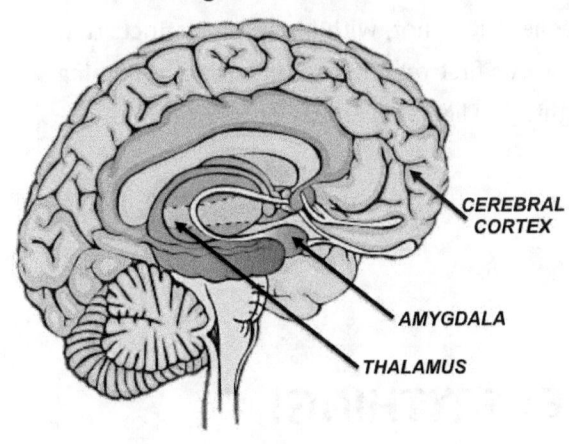

FIGURE 5

What you see here in Figure 5 is the human brain and I want you to focus on just three areas of the brain for the purposes of this book. It will all soon make sense once you understand the core mechanics of this trio where the secrets of success in life and in business are hidden. I call it the TACO (Thalamus, Amygdala, Cortex) – bear with me, I will explain and it will be clear why I am taking you through this section.

The THLAMUS plays a pivotal role in your brain and is responsible to collect all the sensory inputs from your five senses and relay it to the AMYGDALA first, enroute to the CEREBEAL CORTEX. Some die-hard neuro-scientists claim that this relay occurs in parallel while some claim a serial relay. My research and personal logical interpretation of this matter coming from my engineering background prompts me to believe we have primarily more of a series circuit than a parallel circuit going on here. Both circuits are active simultaneously from a 'wiring' perspective but it is the individual's personal neuro-conditioning that ultimately dictates whether the captured impulse will even get past their over-powering Amygdala to even fire the neurons in the Cerebral Cortex.

Ah, the AMYGDALA – a glorified medical name for our reptilian brain! For a while I believed that we were descended from monkeys (granted some people out there in the world today, do put our ape ancestors to shame with their caveman-like behavior in the modern day world). So we are at the core, reptiles believe it or not, with four core instincts that naturally give us the ability of our first reaction to any impulse coming from the THALAMUS – (1) Fight, (2) Flight, (3) Freeze or (4) Faint.

Let's test this out for you.

STOP EVERYTHING!

Check your email right now. Seriously, check your email right now.

You have been **hacked** !!!

Yes, *YOU* HAVE BEEN HACKED !!!

Gotcha! Or did I? Apologies for all that drama. Relax, everything is fine (I hope). It was a drill. But how did you react when you read that sentence about getting hacked? That first reaction my friend, is coming from your AMYGDALA. Depending on how you are wired, you might have seriously believed that you were hacked. You might have dropped this book, got mad, maybe even cursed out loud and immediately opened up your email to check if that catastrophe that you have been dreading about has actually caught up with you. Ah, that makes you wired to be more dependent on the reptilian part of your brain than the cerebral cortex. There's nothing to be ashamed of, although if that's how you are wired, we've got work to do as it may very well be adversely impacting your personal life, your social life and your business.

Ah! Now we might have identified a potential problem and are planning to fix it. Enter the CEREBRAL CORTEX. This part of the brain is where your rationality, your intelligence, your analytical ability and reasoning abilities exist. While the Amygdala makes you react to impulses, the Cerebral Cortex helps you to **respond** – big difference.

In that test we just did, when you read that sentence about getting hacked, your Amygdala got triggered first. However instead of that knee jerk reaction, you could have just continued reading unperturbed. Your wiring took you past the barrier posed by the Amygdala and carried the impulse to your Cerebral Cortex for a rational decision to be made. It is impossible for me writing this book days before it landed in your hands to know with so much absolute certainty that your email has been compromised. That's your Cerebral Cortex reasoning for you with the ultimate decision or **response** to just ignore this impulse and move on.

To summarize, the THALAMUS relays the impulse captured from your five senses to the AMYGDALA. Only when you are able to get past the first reaction of AMYGDALA can that impulse get referred to the CEREBRAL CORTEX for analysis and intelligent response. It is this cerebral cortex that makes us human, distinguishing ourselves from other members of the animal kingdom in this planet.

Another concept that you need to understand about the human brain is that it's a highly sophisticated pattern recognition system. When your five senses pick up an impulse, the Thalamus relay records that pattern to memory. The longer you stay in the experience of that pattern, physically and emotionally, deeper is that pattern in your memory.

For example, if I asked you to remember the faces of everyone you 'saw' in the mall the last time you were there, you would probably draw a blank – that is short term memory. They passed you by, your thalamus did its job, but since you were not involved in a prolonged experience with everyone your short-term memory recycled and erased it for some new future data.

However, if I asked you to describe the logo of your company, you would instantly visualize it and vividly describe it for me as if it was right in front of you. Why? Repetition, total immersion with your emotions when you designed it and prolonged exposure to the experience had transferred that impulse from your short-term memory to long-term memory. Your brain recognizes that logo as a specific pattern and can feed it to your Amygdala and the cortical brain instantly and accurately.

With this basic understanding of how the brain works, here's the key takeaway for you. Your objective as a small business owner is to allow impulses to get to the cortical brain as soon as possible, without the reptilian reactions of the Amygdala clouding your intellect, reasoning and rationality. Don't get me wrong, the Amygdala is important – its job is to keep us safe. So a long-term pattern that would be a threat to your safety will be reacted upon right away by your Amygdala, triggering one of those 4 FFFF reactions I mentioned earlier.

However, what is safety? It's what keeps you in the most comfortable state of mind and keeps the Amygdala on standby. The moment you venture out of this comfort zone, the Amygdala is the first to raise an objection. Why? Because it cannot find a stored pattern of that impulse in your memory. The Amygdala has no rationality, no intelligence – just a set of 4 pre-programmed algorithms that repeat over and over. Foreign patterns transferred from the Amygdala are considered a threat to your safety and it flares up with a reaction.

If you are conditioned to be Amygdala-dominant, quite candidly you need to re-think your life story because I can almost guarantee that you are leaving goldmine after goldmine of opportunity on the table as a small business owner for your competition to pick up. Now you understand which part of the brain is prominent for naysayers and pessimistic people. What are they thinking? Or Not ?

Still with me? Looks like you are not mad at me yet – good, and I did not expect you to be mad at me. As small business owners who are writing our own destiny, I think you and I have that Amygdala of ours on a leash as it should be. We take risks, sometimes calculated, sometimes just based on our gut feel – that is a cortical brain response. It is always willing to learn new patterns, define response patterns on those patterns, evolving them further and staying hungry for more of that juice. However, there are times in business when doubts creep in, repeated shortcomings seem to knock us off course. We've all been there – some yield to such storms in life and in business, while some reach the shore battered and bruised but dancing in the arms of victory.

Go Cerebral Cortex !

This background of the human brain brings us to the discussion of your Mindset as a Business Owner, the Skillset and ultimately the Actionset of your entire business ecosystem. I want you to understand the dance between these three fundamental components of your business. I want you to understand that it is **YOUR** Mindset that orchestrates the other two. Then, my friend you will be ready to walk the hallowed hall of fame of frontrunners in your industry. This game of cashflow will then be yours to command and win.

SETTING YOUR MINDSET

Hopefully you are beginning to understand that this mindset thing is not all Woo-Hoo after all. So what's mindset got to do with your cashflow situation? Ah! Welcome to the New Age of running a fluid business, and for some reason, they don't teach this yet in business school.

Mindset is everything. It is your internal GPS. What you want to do is create a string of patterns so deeply etched in your long-term memory that you become *unconsciously competent* about it and your business literally starts to run on cruise control. That string of patterns that I am talking about can be related to anything you choose. For the purpose of this book, we will keep everything focused on the "2X Cashflow in 6 Months" topic.

What is *unconscious competence*? you may be asking. There are 4 levels of learning and your objective in life and in business is to move from Level 1 to Level 4 in order to maximize the knowledge and start to apply it confidently. Here are the levels :

1. **Level 1 – Unconscious Incompetence** : This is where you don't know what you don't know. For example, there's a whole lot more about the human brain that I have not discussed in this Chapter and you don't know what they are.
2. **Level 2 – Conscious Incompetence** – This is where you know what you don't know. For example, before reading this Chapter, you probably knew that you did not know anything about the human brain.

3. **Level 3 – Conscious Competence :** At this level, you know what you know. For example, I have not discussed everything possible about the human brain but you know about what I have discussed, so you are consciously competent about those areas of knowledge.
4. **Level 4 – Unconscious Competence :** At this level, you know what you know so well, it is deeply etched as long term memory in your brain and you don't even need to think about it. It's on auto-play all the time instantly that impulse comes in anytime for processing.

ACTION ALERT : So let's create a pattern for your brain right now and specifically for your Mindset to set the stage for the rest of the book and beyond in your life and business. Get a clean sheet of white un-ruled paper and a blue ink pen. No, any other colored pen or paper will not work, and neither would typing on a computer or gadget – I am adamant about it.

Ready ? Now fill in the blanks and write out the full sentence in your own handwriting (just like a déjà vu to 3rd Grade). Ok, it's silly but will you just do it anyways just for giggles ? Be careful about #3 – dig deep. On #12 and #13, I want you to think about numbers that are believable given your current beliefs and circumstances and then DOUBLE that number before you write that down.

1. I am the successful owner of my business _____.
2. I create / provide _____ to my customers.
3. I am in business because _____.
4. My most ideal customer has the following characteristics _____.
5. The highest value I willingly provide to my most ideal customer is _____.

6. My most ideal employee has the following characteristics _____.
7. The highest value I willingly provide to my most ideal employee is _____.
8. My most ideal business partner has the following characteristics _____.
9. The highest value I willingly provide to my most ideal business partner is _____.
10. My most ideal supplier has the following characteristics _____.
11. The highest value I willingly provide to my most ideal supplier is _____.
12. In 12 months from now, I can taste, touch, smell, see and hear a net revenue of _____ in my business. With this achievement, I feel absolutely _____.
13. In 6 months from now, I can taste, touch, smell, see and hear a net cashflow of _____ in my business. With this achievement I feel absolutely _____.
14. In 12 months from now, I can taste, touch, smell, see and hear _____ happening in my personal life. With this achievement, I feel absolutely _____.
15. In 12 months from now, I can taste, touch, smell, see and hear _____ happening in my relationships. With this achievement, I feel absolutely _____.
16. Overall I deeply feel emotions of _____ in my life filled with purpose, success, happiness, love and peace.

Now that you have completed this exercise, write this down at the bottom "I _____, hereby willingly and without coercion, sign this contract with me and pledge my commitment to honor everything I have written. It is my bond from today onwards."

Now I want your full signature and date it in the bottom. Read the entire document one more time slowly and I want you to feel the emotions, really feel the emotions as you read each sentence. Place this document where you can access it every day. At least once a day for the next 90 days at a minimum – without fail and without any excuses or blame, I want you to read it loud to your self moving your finger over the paper as you read it. Do this repetition at the same time every day almost like unconsciously heading the shower in the morning.

Now, this is getting really Woo-Hoo, isn't it? BEWARE of that over-protective Amygdala, my friend. You are about to set a foreign pattern in your brain and it is natural for the Amygdala to resist. The question is, will you yield or will you ask it to shut that blabbermouth and present that pattern to the Cerebral Cortex to register? We small business owners writing our own destiny don't yield easily, do we?

This isn't some fluff stuff by any stretch of imagination. By playing along with me, going through this exercise and repeating it diligently for the forthcoming 90 days, you will graduate from a state of unconscious incompetence to unconscious competence. The Amygdala is a beast and it can be tamed and so it will through this repeated barrage every day as your cerebral cortex becomes more and more aligned to the new pattern and defines your new mindset.

If you are able to do this diligently, something 'magical' starts to happen. Medical Science cannot explain it, woo-hoo cannot explain the logic, organized religion cannot understand it by any logical stretch of imagination other than giving all the credit to the Supreme Power. But something truly seemingly magical starts to happen.

When you diligently follow this Pattern Setting And Recognition procedure (I call it PaStReP), inexplicable shifts start to occur in your experience in life and in business, precisely along the lines that you have written down. Some call it 'magic', some call it 'miracle'. I call it **Physics**

– pure basic 8th grade Physics. Remember resonant frequencies from school days? If you don't, read up on it and you will understand exactly what I mean. It's resonance, my friend. If you looking for more a more detailed description of the phenomena of these shifts that occur, you may want to peruse my Amazon bestseller "*Oh My Genetics Of Divinity*". But let's get back to the content of this book for now.

Your brain is a transmitter and receiver of electromagnetic frequencies – medical science has proven that for a fact. When you wrote that down in your own handwriting you had triggered an ideo-motor response in your brain. The alphabets that you wrote, the pattern of scratching sounds of the pen on paper, the pattern in which your finger was holding the pen and the pattern of movements your hand was making to write everything down – everything was being recorded first in short term memory. For sure it was a foreign pattern and like it was supposed to, the Amygdala perked up and raised the alarm.

When you read it aloud the first time and then you repeat that ritual every day for 90 days, the pattern upgrades from short term to long term memory and it becomes part of your internal knowledgebase. When you do that ritual, you will find after 7-10 days, you may not need to even have the paper in front on your to read. You can playback from memory without any dropouts. When that happens, you have gained conscious competence. Continued repetition beyond that time leads you to the stage of unconscious competence and that pattern starts to affect your thoughts and even your dream states when you sleep.

At this stage, your brain switches from receiving mode to transmitting mode and that pattern starts to emit like sinusoidal waveforms from your brain – specifically the pre-frontal cortex. That's when those frequencies seek out similar sinusoidal frequencies to find a match and engage on a resonant relationship. People, circumstances, events that were in your unconscious incompetence domain start to make themselves known to you, entering your conscious competence state. The Amygdala does its job but the repetition of the pattern weakens its effect and you start to use your rationality, intelligence and powers of analysis to consider these new impulses in your life experience and take appropriate action.

Once these impulses and influences start coming into your life, you know exactly what skills you need, what resources you need to tap into, what forthcoming action steps are needed to meet your objectives. This is how your Mindset, identifies and defines the Skillset that you need to derive the Actionset necessary to meet your objectives you fixated on.

I hope you understand this is not Woo-Hoo stuff any more – its pure science. Actually a combination of neuro-science and laws of Physics is behind this so-called inevitable phenomena that comes into your experience when you follow PaStReP.

I could write for pages and pages on this topic but let's move on with the rest of the content of the book. If you have skipped the exercise, my recommendation to you is that you go through it exactly as I have described and start the process right now as you go through the rest of the content.

I have already suggested some Action Items in the previous chapters to improve your cashflow situation - those were Actionsets. Chances are they did not register with you just yet. Why? Because I intentionally placed the cart before the horse. Actionset before the Mindset and sure enough it did not work, did it? Thankfully those were just some leaky faucets, the minors – again on purpose. As we now get into the majors of new age cashflow management strategies, please ensure that you have completed the Mindset exercise first for maximum benefits of the content coming up next.

5 INNOVATION OR CONDEMNATION
YOUR CUSTOMERS ARE HUNGRY AND THEY CAN PAY

If you procrastinate in your plans to innovate on the product or service line of your business, you can be almost certain that you will lose out to the competition. When that happens, your business will continue to lose market share and we all know what happens when that happens. Dropping revenues erode the net liquidity portion of the Cashflow equation. To compensate, you attempt to expedite your product release at much higher costs, which adds to the net liability component of the Cashflow equation - a double whammy.

Not at all a good position to be as you can imagine. So isn't it just easier on everyone that you have a well-defined strategy of innovation on your line of products and services? Follow the plan and execute on that strategy diligently in order to stay competitive in the market.

Without taking names, you will be surprised how even Fortune grade companies with long and drawn out lead times to market suffer billions of dollars in losses, yielding the market to the competition. When their product finally hits the sales channels, they are met with lukewarm or even cold response from the market. Why? Because the market has already been saturated by the competing product and has already vested their spending dollars on that product line. This is the early mover advantage that Fortune grade companies compete for all the time and as a small business owner you may want to consider this even more seriously.

Why? While Fortune grade companies have the cushion of cashflow to sustain such setbacks, typical small businesses don't have such flexibility. Depending on the size of your niche and the number of competitors in your market, it is imperative that you remain proactive with your innovation strategy and not reactive to competitor launches.

Your market is hungry for the next shiny object, especially if you are a tenant in the consumer goods industry. They wield the spending capacity (even if plastic currency must be used) for the right product that meets as many of the following core emotional triggers (I call them CETs):

1. Specific problem it solves or prevents danger to life and property (Amygdala marketing)
2. Fear of loss or damage (Amygdala marketing)
3. Triumph of possession – especially for limited edition releases
4. Coolness factor and efficacy
5. Pride of association with a brand
6. Simplify bare necessities of modern day life
7. Enhances quality of life and property
8. User-friendliness and simplicity of user interface
9. Cost of acquisition and maintenance
10. Quality, durability and longevity

How many of these emotions does your upcoming product or service address? Greater the better. How long will it take your team to bring that product or service to market for commercial sale? How does that timeline compare with the release schedule of your competition? Fortune Grade companies sometimes have ways and means to find out competitor schedules of product and service release in the same niche. This intelligence however is usually not accessible to the limited budget of small businesses. Having said that the playing field is level if your competitor is also another small business – they have the same dynamics as you . However if the David in your business is to take on the Goliath of a larger company, you better make sure that your innovation addresses more of the consumer emotional factors than Big Brother and that you are releasing before they do.

Regularly scheduled product releases is a must for your small business to keep your market engaged and eager for the next forthcoming release as you continue to raise the benchmark of what value for money the customer can enjoy. **You must be the cause of the effect** products or services have in your niche. That's what sets you apart in the market as the early mover. That's what keeps your competitors guessing your next move. That's what attracts the loyalty of your customer base and that's what generates the big bucks to beef up your cashflow.

WHAT TO INNOVATE

My clients often ask me, "*What can I innovate on?*" Depending on your niche, you may have scratched your head on this one, let alone coming up with pre-planned product or service development lifecycle. My answer is always the same.

1. What can you create to make a **compelling** Unique Selling Proposition (USP) for your consumers?
2. What does the market currently not have at all or can be better than what's already available?

3. What are your customers looking for that hits on their CETs?
4. What can you create something so innovative that it will break the market making you the early mover?
5. What current presenting problem does that product or service solve in the market?
6. What is the cost to the customer of not solving the problem?
7. What is the investment that a customer would have to make in order to procure your new product or service?
8. How soon can they start to see the benefits to recover the costs and derive value from it?

This may seem daunting at first, but it can be fun and invigorating for you and your team to brainstorm and come up with innovative ideas that shake and move the market to generate the highest value possible to your consumers. INNOVATE, INNOVATE, INNOVATE.

Without a doubt, Innovation has a huge impact on your cashflow. One of the core human desires is Variety - the so-called spice of life. Just think about the last time you upgraded your smartphone. Why did you do that? Think about the new menu at your favorite restaurant that you simply can't wait to get a bite at again. Why do you have that craving? It's INNOVATION.

VALUE BASED INNOVATION

As an engineer and solution architect myself, the very concept of Innovation gets my juices flowing in hyperdrive. That's how we engineers and architects are wired. At the same time I profess and practice **Conscious Entrepreneurship** to my small business clients, as I am about to do now to you, so bear with me. The concept of conscious entrepreneurship comes from my personal belief and philosophy in life. We are here on this planet for the sole purpose of serving and creating value for ourselves and as many other lives that we can touch during our brief lifetime and if possible, even beyond our passage through time.

In case you missed out on the keyword there, it's all about creating "VALUE". When you create that value – not just perceived value but also **intrinsic** value for your market, you get rewarded handsomely. Sales, customer loyalty, market reputation, competitor reverence, cashflow - everything acquires a snowball effect to take you even higher and higher in the echelons of the business world.

Consider Tesla Motors. Consumers are lining up for their cars, despite the fact that they are not cheap and they are more suitable for city driving only - not for long distance. Why? So much value has been created by the brand led by one of the great visionaries of our time, Elon Musk. The perceived and intrinsic value for the consumer far exceeds the price they pay, which is why Tesla Motors are so successful. What a vision and what an amazing innovation to lead the pack in the market of electric cars !

What I want to impress upon you is the concept of Value Based Innovation, especially as a small business owner to make the most of the opportunity with the limited resources you have access to. Allow me to outline the new age process of creating products and services that can create that high value for your market. This is most suited to small businesses with limited budget and resources for extensive and long-drawn market research.

1. Create a Market Survey using Social Media.
    a. Use social media channels to create a multiple choice survey asking your market some very pointed questions about your current products and services.
        i. What do they like
        ii. What don't they like
        iii. What do they wish you offered in your products

or services
    iv. What can you do to serve them better
    v. If they had a magical wand, what product or service would they absolutely love to enjoy

Facebook works the best for such an exercise in my opinion. By no means is this an endorsement of Facebook over any other one. I use Facebook myself for such purposes and have seen great results for my business and for my clients.

   b. At the end of the survey provide an incentive, with some non-monetary yet tangible value to encourage them to complete the survey. It could be a social cause "When you complete the survey, we will donate $1 per survey to XYZ Charity" – ah, now you have created value for the consumer and for yourself as well.
   c. Now use Facebook Ads to send the survey to everyone in your product geography who has an interest in your products and your niche or the niche where you are contemplating creation and release of your innovation.
   d. Review the results of the survey– this is a goldmine since the market has just told you what they want from you. The demand has already been seeded.
2. Create an internal organizational survey
   a. Start an internal email campaign asking your employees about their ideas of creating new product and service offerings. Give them a deadline with an incentive for the top 3 winners. You are not asking for details, you are asking them to provide the following information:
       i. What problem does the proposed product or service solve in the market
       ii. What other benefits can the product or service

bring to the consumer
iii. Why would such a product or service be considered valuable by the market
iv. What would be a suggested retail price for such a product or service that creates that value
b. Review the results of your survey
c. Organize a brown bag lunch session almost like a corporate event where you announce the winners with some rah-rah speeches from the management.
d. This instills a sense of pride to belong to your business and being credibly heard by the top management – this goes deep into employee loyalty
3. Gather all the creative brains in your organization and analyze the results from #1 and #2. Note, I am not talking about specific products or services – yet. I am just talking about the VALUES. Let's go at a higher level than the intrinsic product or service.
4. Classify the items above as **A, B** and **C** category of values.
   a. "**A**" would be the
      i. highest value it could be to a customer?
      ii. fastest you can release a product or service that creates high value in the market
      iii. least amount of investment (time, money, people) needed to create that value
      iv. least competition in the market
   b. "**B**" would be medium.
      i. It could be valuable, but not extraordinary.
      ii. There may be some competition in the market
      iii. It may take a while to get this product or service for sale in the market
      iv. A fair amount of investment may be necessary.
   c. "**C**" category – well you may not even want to go there, because they are not very valuable, it will take a long time to bring to the market, and by that time , the

competition might have already released something similar and it would require some large investment. In that case it could not be worth pursuing that idea.
5. Eliminate them from the list and now look at "**A**" and "**B**" again and go the process again to come up with another **ABC Analysis** of the leftovers, thereby narrowing the list even further.
6. Ultimately you will come up with the single highest set of values that you can create for the market.
7. Now go design that tangible product or service to create that intrinsic value.
8. Calculate the cost to create that product or service and the suggested price that you would be asking for. Typically anything below a minimum 30% margin, depending on your product or service, needs to go through a vetting process.
9. Estimate the market volume for your innovation
10. Introduce the product or service into its Lifecycle and break the market upon release.

NEUROSCIENCE IN INNOVATION

From a neuro-scientific perspective, INNOVATION goes directly into understanding your market's mindset that I will get into in more detail in Chapter 6. Thankfully you are marketing to humans after all – even if you are in the pet products or service market. They have the same brain architecture that primarily works exactly the same as yours. The difference between you and your market is in the patterns that are wired in your brains. I have discussed what your market is looking for. Scan that list again, except the first two, which are prominently to pacify the Amygdala, the others are more to please the more analytical and pleasure seeking cortical brain. Most definitely all of them without exception would need to get past the gates of the Amygdala before it can appeal to the Cortex. So that's your objective as a small business owner when you are in the Innovation path. Pacify the Amygdala and appeal to the Cortex – then rinse and repeat.

Innovation in your products and services breathes in that fresh air and life into your portfolio. The innovation's got to make it easier, better, faster, cheaper and creates more of that "cool-factor" in your customer's mind. They get motivated towards a trade-in or fresh purchase adding to the positive component of the Cashflow formula by way of new sales and net revenue. Higher your sales numbers, needless to say greater is your potential for creating higher cashflow in your business.

Consider Apple – one of the frontrunners in innovation in the technology world today. They create some really cool products for consumer use. They release one product and people storm the stores to stake their claim on the "cool factor". Think about the Quality of Apple's products - think about their packaging - think about the form factor of their products. Innovation is what drives Apple and consumers eagerly await the next Keynote speech announcing the new in-thing in their market.

Innovation must also be done with short conception-to-market lead times. You could have the most exciting product since sliced bread. But if you are not fast enough to bring it to the market for real commercial use, you can bet that your competitor will steal your show and beat you to the chase. If you are unable to generate market demand (at times even if you are creating the emotions for that demand) through an elaborate pre-launch campaign, chances are you will be falling short, regardless of the oomph factor of the product.

Consider Microsoft as compared to Apple. They got beaten to the smartphone market by Apple and even today, Windows phones are 3rd in the smartphone market. Microsoft released Surface® with so much fanfare with such great forecasts and predictions but Apple released the iPad® Mini just before them to capture the imagination, frenzy and favor of consumers. When Microsoft came to the market they found that the market was already saturated with Apple products in the mobile device industry. The consumers had already made their investment in an innovative product with the oomph and coolness of Apple that Microsoft could not topple. The market statistics never lie about the true consumer behavior.

As a small business owner you definitely don't have the cushion of such setbacks that a Microsoft would have which is why you need to be extra vigilant and meticulous about your Innovation strategy. Carefully consider your lead-time of conception-to-market. You must be the early mover in the market with your innovation and get it out in the market as soon as possible. The objective here obviously is to generate more sales and hence higher liquidity for your cashflow equation.

However the cost of being beaten to the finishing line by a competitor with a similar or better product can crush any small business. Why? Because all that cost of innovation, pre-launch and launch marketing, that you would have funded from your cashflow would remain unrealized as you fight to break even on your investment. Ah Innovation - the double-edged sword. Be careful how you swing it in your business.

PROTECT YOUR INTELLECTUAL PROPERTY

Not to sound cocky, but stay vigilant about your innovative ideas, plans and designs. Corporate espionage was not born yesterday in this modern day world of business. I will address Cybersecurity in more detail in Chapter 8, but for the purpose of this Chapter I want to call out this peril of doing business in the new age. Lack of a confidentiality policy or a need-to-know principle for your staff and strategic partners is pivotal to protect your strategic plans for anything in your business. Innovation is no different. If Innovation is going to be a key source and nutrient in the lifeblood of your business, you have to protect that Intellectual Property with all the operational and legal muscle you can bring to muster.

From an operational procedure, employee conduct and also the legal perspective, you must have the right Intellectual Property protection strategies in place when you embark on the high reward road of Innovation. If you have a shiny object coming up that would break the market, rest assured there are people outside your organization who are interested to get a sneak peek at what you've got.

Copyrights and trademarks (or service marks) are easy and cheap to file and secure in almost all countries. But depending on your product or service, these are not enough to secure the Intellectual Property of your Innovation. However filing for a patent can be quite a stretch for small businesses due to the costs involved.

In the United States, you can file for a provisional patent with about a $2000 investment including filing and legal fees. This provisional patent secures a date with the USPTO and starts the more rigid protection process of your Innovation. It also allows you a year of protection until you file for a Utility or a Design Patent within that year. In general terms, a "**utility patent**" protects the way your new product or service will be used and functions (35 U.S.C. 101), while a "**design patent**" protects the way an Innovation appears from a physical characteristics point of view (35 U.S.C. 171).

A utility patent is far more expensive to file and takes longer to be approved by the patent office than a design patent and also offers a much greater protection for your new product than a design patent. For a small business owner it is often a significant challenge to have access to the funds to get the protection of a utility patent or have the energy to go through the elaborate and time consuming filing and approval process.

It is becoming increasingly difficult to get software applications and mobile apps approved for a Utility Patent from the USPTO because it is quite challenging to prove uniqueness in the fast moving world of software. I am sure you are facing the same kind of reluctance in your country if you are not from the USA.

Be very careful and perform a significant amount of research before you file for software patent (or any patent for that matter). Patent attorneys have established very lucrative careers defending or petitioning for Patent violations. For a small business these costs may be insurmountable. What do we do as small business owners? Perform extreme due diligence before you go for the patent route. For sure you can have a patent attorney perform the due diligence to determine uniqueness of your Innovation and in most cases this is advisable just to be sure. But it does not hurt for you and your Innovators to do some digging yourself first.

However when you file the provisional patent application you are granted the right by the USPTO to use "Patent Pending" in all public announcements of your new Innovation. It gives you that one year of protection right from the date of filing that provisional patent application. Very cool. Please research the laws in your country if you are not from the United States.

That "Patent Pending" gives you breathing space for a year and if you don't file for a utility and/or design patent within that year, you lose that right and your Innovation becomes open game. Depending on how much is already in the public domain, expiration of your rights could imply a vulture feast for your competition. All that hard work and all that investment of time, money and energy is literally a write off. OUCH, a big one for your cashflow for sure.

After that initial $2000 for the provisional patent, prepare for anywhere between a low five to low six figures in total costs for the Utility patent application, depending on the Innovation. Yup it's tough for small business owners but that's what you are up for, my friend.

Now that you understand the parameters at play here are some suggestions for you to consider, assuming that you do intend to protect your Intellectual Property from being claimed by the competition.

- Do you really need to file a patent or is it more of your ego clouding your emotions? I told you that some of the content in this book can be a little difficult to swallow. No offense. I have been a victim of this same ego myself and have taken the hit to learn lessons the hard way.
- Is your Innovation so very unique that you believe there is nothing close it in the market? This is what the Patent Authority will evaluate anyway and will absolutely reject your application if they think your invention is not unique enough.
- Do you have access to the funds to go through the entire long-drawn process of getting your product Patent Approved? Remember the uniqueness test – the Patent Award Authority in your country (eg. the USPTO in the United States) can simply deny your patent application regardless of all the fees you might have already paid to file for the patent.
- Is your product or service lifecycle long enough to even require protection after the patent is approved? If the product life cycle is say 3 years for example before a better version hits the market and the patent process takes 5 years to get approved, is there a justification to even file for the patent?
- Why bother all the expenses if your Innovation has a shorter lifecycle and you will be releasing a better product or service upgrade anyway within the period where your application is still

pending with the Patent office?
- Can you file the Provisional, release that product or service within that one year, make enough net revenue, generate enough cashflow to fund that Utility and/or Design Patent ? This is of course if you really have to file for a patent.
- Can you convince a Venture Capital firm or corporate investor to fund your Utility/Design Patent in exchange of equity in your company ?
- Could you Crowdfund your Utility/Patent Application? You must get your Provisional Patent filed before you embark on this crowdfunding route. This keeps your Innovation protected and yet can potentially get you access to the larger funds necessary. Consider this very viable New Age strategy seriously. Well-designed Crowdfunding campaigns generate great rewards.

INNOVATE, INNOVATE, INNOVATE. When you are done, learn the lessons, take corrective action and repeat the process to create more value for your market.

6 READING YOUR ECOSYSTEM'S MINDSET
KNOW YOUR ECOSYSTEM AND YOU WILL RULE YOUR INDUSTRY

I am certain that by now you are more convinced than ever before that creating higher cashflow in your organization is much more than just an accounting function. There are several influencers in your business that impact the new effect they have on your net cashflow. Unless your business has you as the only customer, you are operating in an ecosystem in the market. Understanding the mindset of this ecosystem and adapting your operations and business strategies to factor in each mindset, is of prime importance when it comes to creating a steady cashflow through your business.

In Figure 6, you will find a schematic describing the four major components of your business ecosystem, each with their core objectives of associating with your brand. For the sake of completeness, there is a fifth ecosystem comprised of the Legal and Regulatory Compliance enforcement agencies that have their own demands and obligations for you to comply with. For the purpose of this book, we will focus on these four components of your ecosystem to understand how managing each of these have a direct impact on your cashflow situation in the new age of busines management. Part of your own Mindset development must be to acknowldge the mindset of this ecosystem and how you can

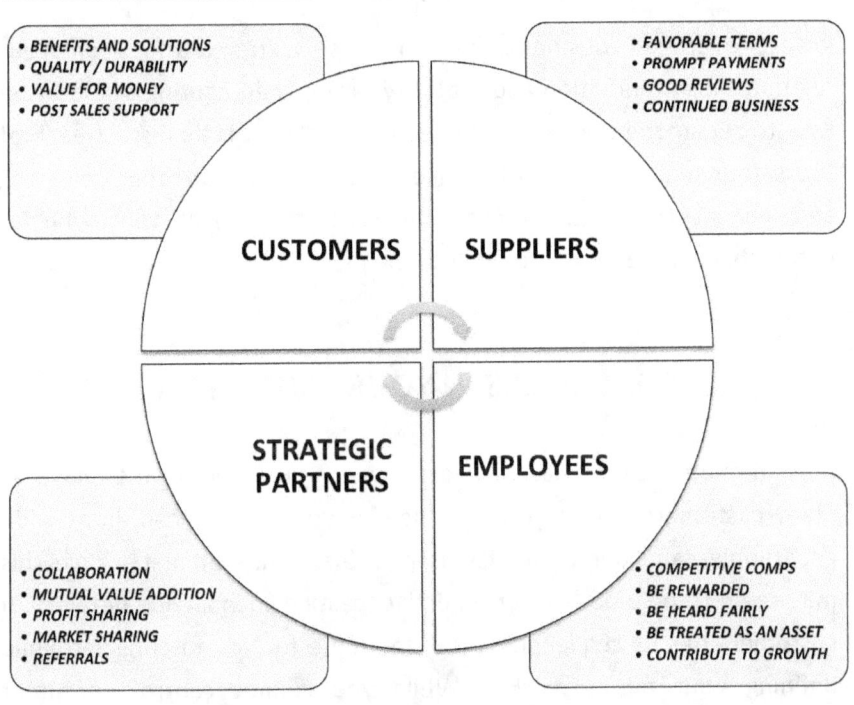

FIGURE 6

accommodate their objectives to derive the most value of this each such relationship.

Consider this as a marriage where each party is required to understand the basic tenets of the relationship, set expectations of each other, honor and nurture these expectations in order to grow and evolve in the spirit of symbiotic collaboration. When these agreed upon expectations are not met, that is when the relationship gets strained. Ultimately that involves additional costs to either take corrective action to make amends or even break the relationship. In effect straining the relationships in any quadrant of your business ecosystem has a direct adverse impact on your net liability portion of the cashflow equation.

As a small business owner with an objective to operate the leanest and lowest overhead business, you must be extra cautious on your relationships at initiation and maturity rather than figuring out later on how to repair the cracks that may come up later. Let's dissect each of these four major tenants of your ecosystem to ensure that you treat and manage them right. Prevention has historically proven to be far better than a cure – traditional or in the new age.

CONSUMERS IN YOUR ECOSYSTEM

Most definitely as a small business owner you would love to have as many customers buying your products as you possibly can, in as wide geographies and demographics as possible. While at first glance this may seem to be a no-brainer objective, casting such a wide network of customers has its challenges. Here are some for you to consider while defining your target market. While you cannot control consumer behavior you can adopt counter-measures to mitigate the risks.

IDEAL CUSTOMER or CLIENT : Do you know who your ideal client or customer is? If not, why not? Take a moment to write down in as precise detail as possible all the characteristics you expect your ideal client or customer to have.

Gender, age, geographical location of residence or transit, income, net worth, language, interests, group affiliations, publications they read, places they visit, religion (believe it or not), services and products they buy, lease or rent, websites they visit, bills they pay, size of family, marital status, type of work they do, their position at work, their academic qualifications, places they lived in the past, employers they worked for, businesses they had or have, creditworthiness. The list can be pretty extensive depending on the market you are in and the value you are creating for that market with your products and services. You MUST know precise characteristics of your most ideal client or customer to understand their MINDSET, so that you can validate your SKILLSET and VALUESET to influence their ACTIONSET. Read that last sentence again till you get it.

Once you have the list of your most ideal client, it's time to make a list of clients and customers that you DON'T want to do business with. It sounds outright crazy at first glance but let me tell you that this segment of your potential market is arguably the biggest risk to your business – period.

In my own consulting company at Go Getter Strategies LLC, I have both of these lists precisely documented and stored along with my important corporate documents and on my desk. All my marketing funnels has in-built filters that measure, analyze and filter out those that do not meet my qualifying criteria of my ideal clients. I do not work with everyone, because first of all I don't have time to waste on a person who does not meet my basic qualifying criteria. It is negative energy for me and the association does not help that client or me. Regardless of the loss of revenue this selection process does, I know I am operating a low risk practice where all my chosen clients are happy, successful and going somewhere fantastic in their lives. I am happy in turn for their success and the contribution I am able to make in their professional and personal lives. As a small business owner myself, I don't have the bandwidth to waste time and every minute wasted on a disgruntled client is a minute that could have made me money from an ideal client.

I encourage you to consider such a filtering mechanism in your client acquisition and retention funnels for your own small business – it will serve you in the long run.

LANGUAGE SUPPORT : If you are marketing to geographies where people primarily speak a language that you and your staff are *"Non comprendo"*, you are setting yourself up for a lot of issues related to customer support, repair and maintenance. These increase your operating costs, unhappy customers, loss of revenue, returns, refunds, chargebacks, negative posts on social media and so on. Every one of these adds to your net liability and decreases your cashflow.

It is just not worth taking the risk of offering products for a market that is such high maintenance, especially for a small business. Bilingual demographics are still ok as long as your customers speak the language that your staff understands. Stay in your niche and serve your customers to the best of your ability. A disgruntled customer, especially in today's new age of social media addiction, is a big threat to your corporate image.

LOGISTICS : Unless you are in the business of selling online software downloads, information products, online training or consulting services, managing the physical product supply chain with both forward and reverse logistics could be quite an overhead for your small business to sustain. If you are as service provider and target customers outside your current geography, you better make sure you have your own competent staff or contractors to serve those demographics. Its not good business sense to get a customer in a different geography in your sales funnel only to let them know that you cannot serve them.

USING YOUR PRODUCT OR SERVICE : Want to cut down on expensive customer support calls? In addition to creating well tested and high quality products and services, you must make sure that you have clear instructions on how you use your product or service. In the new age of business, consumer demographic statistics indicate that printed manuals are ignored and not referenced. Customers prefer online documentation or even better still instructional videos that clearly describe each feature and function of your product and service. This also includes trouble-shooting videos and content that the customer can follow before making that customer service call to you. Do your small business a favor, go through your product and service portfolio and if you have not created rich, descriptive online documentation and instructional videos for use and troubleshooting, just get them done.

In addition, resist the temptation to have your developers create this documentation. These folks typically assume their own level of expertise while creating documentation, which may be quite difficult for an average customer to follow. Use your training staff to create such customer friendly documentation and make them easily searchable and accessible on your website.

Self-serve documentation significantly reduces customer support calls, which saves you on support overheads.

QUALITY : As a small business we are always trying to operate as efficiently and as thriftily as possible. It is not uncommon for us to cut corners in certain aspects of our business. Whatever you do, make it your mantra never to compromise on quality of your products and services. A high quality product costs higher than a lower quality product for sure, but that higher cost typically ensures better and longer performance according to the stated specifications.

If you are a service provider, the more automated your services are, better it is for your operations. Completing the service call in one visit or interaction with the customer needs to be your primary objective. I recommend binding this principle to your performance evaluation metrics of your staff.

High quality products and services that require little maintenance, repair or rework are significantly more profitable than products and services that skimp on quality. Ask yourself the question, would you give your product or service to your loved ones to use? If the answer is 'No' or if there is hesitation in your mind, then chances are that you have a quality issue in your hands that needs to be fixed a.s.a.p. before it spreads out in the market.

Fortune grade companies have to bear the burden of millions and millions of dollars in costs and missed opportunities when they skimp on quality and are forced to make product recalls. Make sure your small business stays clear of such nightmares by ensuring high quality.

Nothing's more important than the name and reputation of your brand in the market and high quality products and services can guarantee customer loyalty and repeat business and keep your social media profile clean and untarnished. Unfortunate as it sounds in this new age of conflict that we live in, people would rejoice your victories once but will talk about your shortcomings for days in social media channels.

TROLLS IN YOUR CUSTOMER BASE : Everything said and done, there will be customers that come through your marketing funnels, who will never ever be happy. To top it off, they will come in to take advantage of your products and services. If you are selling physical products or even digital products, you will find customers who will purchase from you, use it and then take advantage of your trial period to return it back for a refund. These customers consistently live by a use-return-refund policy in life and are definitely a threat to your revenue stream and business cashflow projections.

Some of these trolls in your consumer base may even move from store to store recycling your product every 30 days, enjoying all the benefits of your generous 30 day money back guarantee. Yup, as a conscious small business owner and entrepreneur, such behavior sounds unbelievable. Ask any consumer electronics manufacturers and retail outlets and you will know how serious this problem can be.

Note that if you are offering these trial periods (if you are in the US, you need to provide this anyway), although you have the money you cannot recognize that revenue as earned revenue. It needs to stay in your books as deferred revenue until the trial period is over when you can claim that money as your own asset.

What is the solution to such a problem of habitual use-return-refund-repeat customers who take advantage of your generosity and the laws of the land? This is a tough one due to the unpredictability of this problem in your sales channel. But technology can help when implemented properly and consumer purchase systems are integrated well with purchase behavior tracking systems. The specifications of such a track-follow-adjudicate pattern detection and warning system is beyond the scope of the book. I will be happy to work with you if you are experiencing such a problem in your sales channels.

The last thing you want in your consumer ecosystem is a Public Relations fiasco on social media that goes viral. So pick your target market carefully based on their MINDSET and your SKILLSET, your VALUESET to create that favorable ACTIONSET to acquire and retain customers and clients who you would love to serve and work with.

SUPPLIERS IN YOUR ECOSYSTEM

Whether you are a product manufacturer or a service provider, in all likelihood you are relying on suppliers for your components and contracted services that make up your final product or service. From a customer point of view, they hold **you** accountable for the quality of what ever it is that you are selling, not your supply chain. You are the only responsible and accountable party to your customers, not your suppliers. They don't care about your excuses, they don't care about you transferring the blame on your suppliers for the non-performance of your product or service offerings. Essentially, while suppliers are required for your business, they are also a high-risk relationship for your business. Your brand reputation is on the line and as small business owner that is the most valuable asset of your business.

While I hate to dig up old dirt, I can't help remember the huge recalls Ford Motor Company were forced to do because the Goodyear tires in their cars started to fail on the road causing accidents. It crippled the reputation of both Ford and Goodyear and took them years to recover from that catastrophe. Remember the story when a malfunction in the design of the parking brake system of a Dodge caravan took it off park as the van rolled down to crush a toddler who was playing behind it. I wonder if Dodge has recovered fully from it. Such stories are not uncommon and major corporations all have similar battle stories to tell.

As a small business you simply cannot afford such events to occur because a supplier did not hold up their side of the terms of the contract. The blame game simply does not work. You need to be vigilant in your supplier selection process. Figure 6 illustrates what your Suppliers are expecting from you. Similarly, you need to have clear language in your purchase contract what you expect from them in return so that the relationship is a mutually beneficial partnership.

Here's a checklist of action steps for due diligence that you must perform on a regular basis – at least annually to ensure that you are continually qualifying your suppliers to keep them on their toes. Skimp on this and you could be operating with a potential risk in your business.

- Create a supplier intake funnel in your business just like you would create marketing funnels in your business.
- Go through a RFI (Request For Information) process for a first round of eliminations, followed by a RFP (Request For Proposal) process with the first round qualifiers only, to pick however many you need for your supply chain.
- Interview them personally to fully understand their MINDSET,

SKILLSET, VALUESET and ACTIONSETS. Ignore the sweet talk, focus on the core of what you expect.
- Test them on their familiarity of exactly what you require them to do for your business.
- Ask for references and actually contact their references for feedback on how credible these shortlisted suppliers really are.
- Review their websites, search engines and social media profiles, if they have any, to analyze content that you may find.
- Obtain a copy of their Certificate of Good Standing from the Secretary of State in their state of incorporation.
- Search their public records in their state of incorporation for any red flags.
- If they are a public company, you have access to a ton of information that you can access freely.
- Ask them about their own supply chain.
- Inquire them about their own manufacturing processes and quality management controls in place. Are they compliant with any standards from the ISO or similar standards institution?
- Ask them about their employee hiring process. Do they perform background checks on their employees and contractors?
- Perform background checks on them.
- Read all contracts carefully and negotiate terms that are mutually balanced from an accountability and responsibility perspective, especially in the areas where you talk about the "Non-conformance" clause.
- Once they are in business with you, monitor the quality of their products and the timeliness of delivery for your assembly line. How many units are failing to perform according to specs on the assembly line and/or in the field? How frequently? What impact did that failure have on your production lead times and customer satisfaction? How many customer complaints can be attributed directly to the supplier? Can you prove it?
- Create a suppler profile and maintain all of these performance

metrics for analysis at the end of the contracted period.
- If you have multiple suppliers for related components or services, perform a supplier analysis every year and come up with an A, B, C rating for each one of them.
- Renegotiate terms diligently and periodically to keep suppliers on their toes - move them around. Take them off your supply chain if they are consistently under-performing.

As a small business owner you simply cannot afford to take the risk of having a problem in your supply chain. One bad complaint from a customer can be serious enough for your business from a reputation, revenue, overhead costs and hence cashflow perspective. Stay vigilant and proactive while managing your supply chain.

STRATEGIC PARTNERS IN YOUR ECOSYSTEM

I cannot stress enough how important strategic partnerships are for your small business to establish and scale your footprint in the market without bearing all the overheads of marketing by yourself.

TEAM, Together Everyone Achieves More. Instead of going all alone by yourself, think about what strategic partnerships can you forge with other companies who have COMPLEMENTARY products and services. Such a partnerships can significantly help you collectively generate higher value to your customers by bundling your products and services together to create win-win-win offerings in the market.

I call this **ECOSYSYTEM BRIDGING**, which allows you build connections between your market and the market of these strategic partners. This allows you to enter markets that might not have been in your radar before. Such strategic partnerships can lead to increased revenues for both parties in your respective markets and in the bridged market with increased revenues for both parties. They promote your products in their market and you promote for them in your market - this is bi-directional leverage.

Think about this - your sales force can just double or even quadruple without spending an additional dime, depending on how big that strategic partnership is. More revenue from the bridged market at no extra cost of marketing. – how important is that for stretching your cashflow numbers?

Your partners have their own marketing budget just like you do. When you combine products and services, you can optimize these budgets or even achieve more. Neither of you have to go out of the way to promote the other and yet you generate more sales collectively. Your mutual customers enjoy more value for their money from your complementary products and services.

Strategic partnerships can also spark new ideas for innovative products that you can create for the bridged ecosystem. This can also contribute to increased market share, which contributes to your cashflow. What should be the cost of maintaining this strategic partnership? Miniscule or should be miniscule, otherwise it is not a strategic partnership.

How do you find and create these Strategic Partnerships? Research and due diligence is the key as always.

When your customers buy your products and services, what other related products and services do they also buy? You would need to do some research on that. Depending on what you are selling, you could go to Amazon or eBay and search on a product. Pick a product and then Amazon or EBay would give you a list of suggested products that buyers have also purchased or searched in addition to the original product.

Along the same lines, you need to perform a similar research with your product or service - of course I am not saying you have to sell on Amazon or EBay. Your sales and marketing team may already have these insights on up-sell or cross-sell product lines.

You are looking for complementary products and services not competitive - this is very important for you to understand. ***you are looking for complementary products and services NOT competitive***. Why? Because the objective here is to forge strategic partnerships and you don't usually create such partnerships with a competitor to gain market share, do you?

It should be quite straightforward for you to come up with such a list of complementary products and services. Now research and list the top 5 market leaders for each of the complementary products and services that you have identified. Who are these market leaders from a market share perspective? Research their social media pages and see what kind customer comments and feedback they are getting in the market. Perform a Google or Bing search on their name and view the pages on the first two pages of the search engine results. Are there any blog posts about them? What are people saying about their products and services? Are they in a reputation management site like Yelp? Don't forget to check www.pissedconsumer.com and www.ripoffreport.com. Is there any content in these sites? If yes, what are people saying and how serious are those negative comments? Do you think they are from real people or from trolls?

Now make a shortlist of these partners based on their market presence and popularity. If you want to expand your business in another geography or demography, find such partners in those geographies and demographics who can introduce your products and services in those bridged markets.

In order to have a consistent and repeatable process I highly recommend that you assign a dedicated resource to create and manage a structured Strategic Partnership program. This must include the following components :

1. A Partner Outreach strategy,
2. A Communications component – both internally and with the partner,
3. Legal terms and conditions of the collaborative partnership (consult with a competent lawyer of course),
4. Clearly articulate what value you bring to your partner and what value you expect from them in return.
5. Are there any financial aspects of the partnership? Ideally there should not be any, but if there are, note them down as an item of negotiation.
6. How are you going to support them in promoting your products to their market ?
7. How can you support marketing their products in your market?
8. What would be the combined compelling USP in your bridged market?
9. What kind of messaging and communication will each of you have with your individual and mutual customer base, in your websites and social media channels so that the consumers in the bridged ecosystem can see the higher value you collectively bring to them ?
10. Will you make a joint Press Release (yes, you must)? What would be the content of that Press Release.

If you have a compelling USP in your products and services then such strategic partnerships are not too difficult to find and establish, especially when no financial commitment or investment is essential.

I want to refer you back to Figure 5 and to our earlier discussions on the how the human brain functions. Here too, you need to get past the gates of your chosen partner's Amygdala before you can appeal to their Cerebral Cortex with all the rationality and reasoning, why it makes so much sense to create that strategic partnership. Just like any other segment of your Ecosystem, feed that WIIFM (What's In It For Me) message to your partner as early as you can in the process of structuring such relationships.

EMPLOYEES IN YOUR ECOSYSTEM

Unless you are solopreneur in your small business I am certain you are aware that employees are your most valuable asset in the business. The quality, skillset, dedication, performance of your employees literally ensures that the lights stay on in your business. Everything we have discussed so far would be redundant theory, if you did not have the qualified Intellectual Capital in your business to implement that theory into practice.

As a small business owner, finding the properly motivated employee and being able to retain them long enough to serve in your business is of prime importance. You don't have much bandwidth for too much turnover in your Intellectual Capital in a small business. Each time you hire and terminate an employee you have to deal with a learning curve before the new hire can come up to speed and resume from where the earlier employee left off. Not always can a small business sustain such turnovers, leading to sub-optimal operations that could very well affect your cashflow, depending on the area of your business where the vacancy was created.

Hire the right person for the job and ensure that you understand the Employee Mindset. Stay proactive about meeting all the employee expectations from you as illustrated in Figure 6. Then you can address this employee turnover problem very effectively. Productive and efficient employees may not be easy to come by who agree to your compensation plan. The current corporate climate of mergers and acquisitions, bankruptcies, business closures, uncertainty of growth and staff reduction has also created fear in the mind of the workers. With some solid experience under their belt, qualified resources with a flair for entrepreneurship prefer to go solo to start their own small business.

As a small business owner looking for smart hires, you need to be attractive enough for the mature employee pool to get them to an interview. Needless to say, you must take proactive steps to ensure that your new hire is the right person you are looking for. Ensure you are going through the following steps to hire employees - going beyond the resume and the interview.

- Perform a comprehensive background check. This is a highly recommended practice for all US employers today. For sure there is a cost involved but it is often well worth the upfront investment to ensure that you are not hiring a criminal or someone with questionable histories.
- Check all references, past employers, certifications, diplomas, degrees – thorough background check reports often include such information.
- A lot of false and glorified information of capabilities is being thrown into resumes by candidates these days. Question everything, even if the interview takes longer time.
- If you are not a technical person interviewing a candidate for a technical position, you are at risk of being sweet-talked into. Get a technical person to do the technical interview.
- Phone interviews are ok for preliminary elimination rounds. However for final round of interviews before you make an actual offer of employment, ensure that you have the candidate in person in your premises or over applications such as Skype or Oovoo. I have been bitten by masquerading candidates in the past and those were not pleasant experiences.
- When the candidate is in your hiring funnel in addition to the above, check their social media profiles on all of the popular social media sites. Who are they associating with? What kind of posts are they making? How are they commenting on other

posts? As a certified Social Media Investigation Analyst myself, I can tell you social media sites have become a goldmine of very valuable information in the new age.
- Take them through a personality test during the hiring process to ensure you are hiring a person with the right attitude that fits your corporate culture.
- At your discretion, you may want them to get medically examined as a criteria of hire. While life and longevity cannot be predicted, you want to make sure that you are hiring a fit enough person to be able to perform to your expectations.

Employee retention is a big challenge for small business owners, in this highly competitive market today. The uncertainty of world politics and the instability of the corporate environment is making the talent pool prefer to work for the highest paying employer, even if they have to make a few sacrifices. You may not be able to match a compensation package, but you can create a work environment and culture that energizes and empowers the employees with certain degrees of freedom that they may not enjoy elsewhere. That may be incentive enough for the employee to continue to contribute to your Intellectual Capital and growth.

Make sure that your employees are being heard at all times. Collapse the reporting hierarchy to as flat a structure as possible to eliminate information and corporate objectives being lost in translation. 360° feedbacks and peer reviews are increasing in popularity, adoption and effectiveness to ensure that everyone has a fair playing field, regardless of rank and position in the company. Everyone needs to be responsible and accountable for their individual contribution and be evaluated through at least two performance reviews every year.

Goal setting the old traditional way has become ineffective these days and is considered more of a chore than anything else. Employee goals must be aligned with corporate objectives and not created in vacuum. It is the responsibility of your Executive Leadership Team to communicate the State Of The Business as frequently as possible.

Town Hall style meetings must be organized regularly, where employees are encouraged to participate with innovative ideas, feedback, suggestions, and recommendations. These opportunities for open and honest communication delivered in a flat organization structure, make the modern day tech savvy employee feel that they belong somewhere and are an integral part of a bigger story.

Publicly recognize and encourage not only the winners in your business but everyone else who contributed to that win. Consider an open door policy with your employees to demonstrate that you are one of them when it comes to making your small business roar.

Acknowledge the fact that your average employee is investing a third of their daily quota of hours working for you, making you wealthy and taking you into the limelight. Stay grateful and helpful to them and appreciate their service to make them feel wanted and acknowledged. In a small business such a camaraderie can work wonders for you and promote employee loyalty.

When the time comes to terminate an employee, recognize that you are making a major decision in their life. They may have obligations to meet and a family to feed. It is unprofessional these days and may get you into legal trouble if you go about this termination of employment with an iron hand. It is not uncommon for expensive lawsuits these days against employers for wrongful termination. Take care of their transition plan – refer the employee to a career planning company to assist them to find another job. In a nutshell do everything you can to ensure a smooth transition out of your business.

We have covered all the four major business ecosystems and I believe you understand the Mindset at play in each of these ecosystems. This is the age of symbiotic collaboration, the age of social sharing where news travel faster than you can complete a deep breath. This is the age where the world population is in a lot of physical and mental stress due to the uncertainty in global politics and world economics that are affecting small businesses in many ways. Tensions are high in the corporate world and in the workforce.

As a small business owner, you need to ride along with the changing times, continually adjusting and adapting to the changes in order to operate a net positive cashflow operation. Your entire ecosystem is evolving in the new age and it is imperative that you stay in step or risk yielding the momentum of your business to the proactive competition.

7 RECYCLIC BUSINESS PROCESS RE-ENGINEERING

This Chapter by itself can be a book in its own right and people have created careers in business process re-engineering. Major corporations have spent millions of dollars in process optimization in an effort to make them more efficient and less costly. Why? Business processes have always been the prime suspect of causing disruptions in the supply chain and in the delivery of the final product or service. Hence the drive and focus for business process re-engineering to optimize the processes, reducing waste and hence process overheads.

For your small business, I won't take you through an elaborate multi-million dollar Six Sigma business process re-engineering exercise. You may very well need something to that degree of sophistication for your business. However, let's keep this short and simple for the purpose of this book and our core objective to get you to 2X your business cashflow in the next 6 Months.

The core objective of any business process re-engineering is to intensely focus on the **highest value** producing activities in an effort to make them increasingly more **profitable.** Review the words in bold in the last sentence. Through a simple process optimization exercise that I will guide you through in this book, you will be able to eliminate waste in your business process flows, reducing cost, making the process more efficient, faster and hence more profitable. Collectively such a process optimization and re-engineering exercise will reduce the liability portion of the cashflow equation and consequently increase your net cashflow.

Every process is composed of a sequence of activities. Each activity in a process flow has the following 10 attributes:

1. at least one **actor** (person(s) with specific skills or system(s) with specific functions to perform the activity),
2. an **action** (what is being done in that activity)
3. a **duration** (time it takes to complete the activity)
4. **tools** and **equipment** (needed to perform that activity)
5. **materials** or **components** (needed to be processed upon)
6. an **input** or "**supplier**" from a preceding activity that triggers the current activity (on what is the action performed)
7. at least one **output** or "**consumer**" (the end result or what is created as a result of the activity)
8. a **cost** (sum of labor, tools, equipment, materials, utilities, waste produced)
9. a **value** (what value does the activity create for the next activity to consume in the process chain and for the overall process)
10. **profitability** (difference between #9 and #8)

Some of my clients have said "*I have a cost center for this part of this business, I have salaries to pay, infrastructure to provide, expenses to pay on this particular cost center. It does not generate any revenue. How can I calculate profitability ?*" Who does your cost center serve? "*Oh yes, of course*". So there you go. What value does that cost center create and in order to create that value, what is the cost to maintain that cost center? Just do the math and the difference is the profitability of your cost center. So every activity in your business must have a monetary value attached to it and be measured in terms of profitability.

EXAMPLE OF BUSINESS PROCESS RE-ENGINEERING

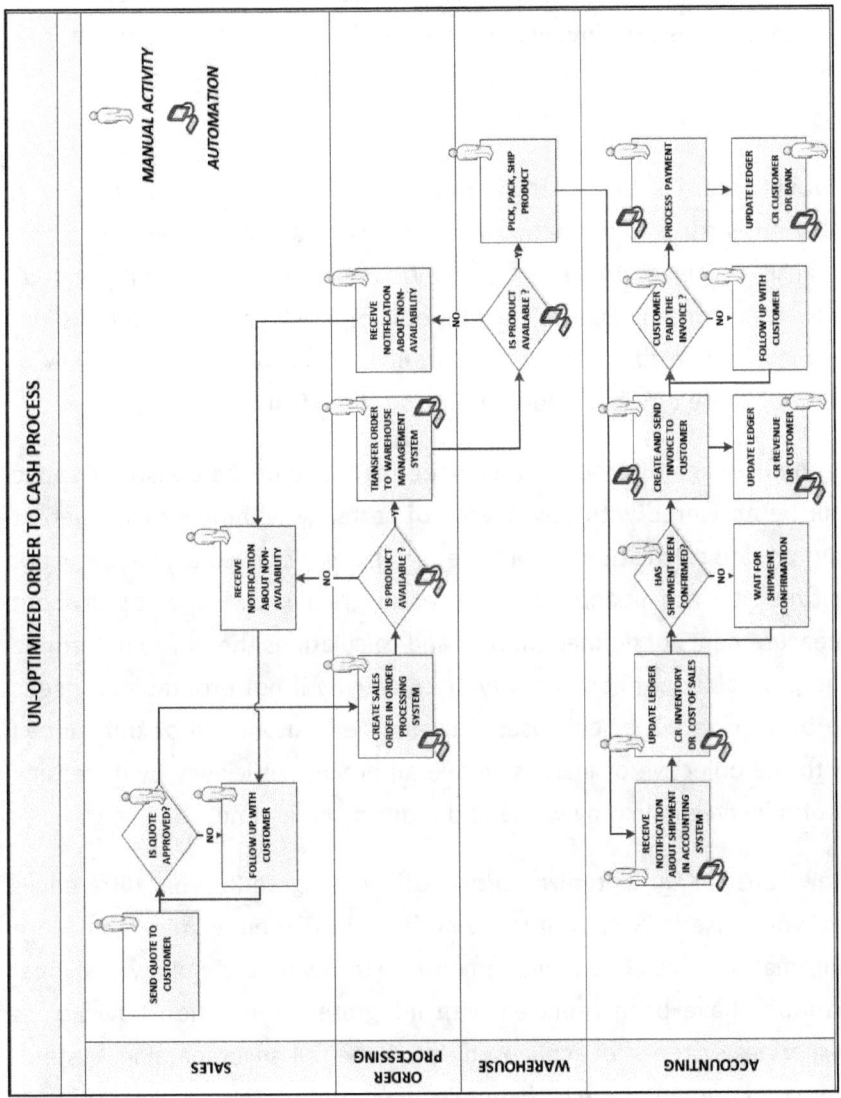

FIGURE 7

Take a moment to carefully analyze the raw and un-optimized business process flow as illustrated in Figure 7, representing a typical **Order To Cash** Process of a business that sells physical products. As you can see there is a lot of manual intervention involved with activities that seem to be repeating over and over again. There are several disconnected automation systems involved that enter the process in different stages. There may as well be manual entry involved by taking data from one system and entering them in the next.

I would hazard a guess that you too are frowning as you review Figure 7. Why on earth would any business have such a complicated and labor-intensive business process? I agree. Why do you think it is complicated? How many areas in Figure 7 in your opinion are high overhead tasks and why? What alternatives can you propose to make the process flow in Figure 7 more efficient? How would you simplify it?

In the new age of process re-engineering, none of the questions above can be answered with any degree of certainly without proper metrics and precise calculations about the profitability of each activity. It is not gut feel, it is not hit and trial, it is also not tribal knowledge. It's all about measurements of defined metrics and calculations thereof to determine the profitability of each activity. If an activity if not profitable, it needs to be eliminated, or collapsed into another, automated or outsourced with the objective of increasing overall process efficiency by increasing profitability, eliminating waste and reducing cycle time.

Now consider the optimized process flow in Figure 8. What differences do you observe? An entire swim-lane has been eliminated. More automation has been implemented through technology. Manual handoffs have been replaced with integrated transaction flow across disparate systems or collapsed into one all-encompassing system. Human intervention has been retained only when it is absolutely necessary. The process flow in Figure 8 has more predictability with built in automated intelligence at each decision step and does not allow subsequent steps to start unless the preceding step has every piece of data required as input for the next step to get kicked off.

NEW AGE STRATEGIES TO 2X YOUR BUSINESS CASHLOW IN 6 MONTHS

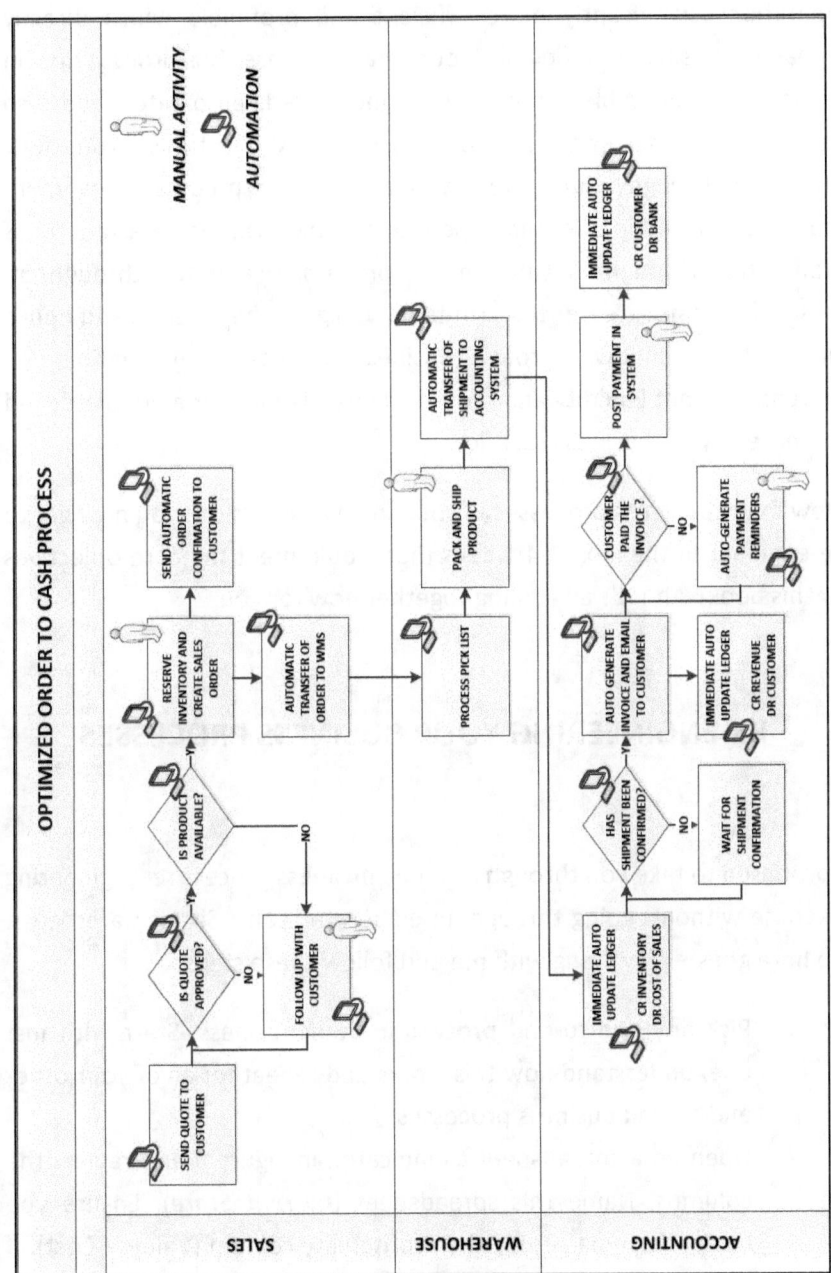

FIGURE 8

So as you can observe, business process re-engineering can make your operations significantly more efficient and profitable which directly impacts a positive cashflow for your small business. This process flow in Figure 8 is adaptable, measureable, monitored, automated and also repeatable for faster transaction processing. When transactions flow smoothly through your system you are able to process many more transactions within the same period of time. This is referred to as transaction throughput through the process. Higher the throughput, lesser the waste, greater the profitability, higher the revenue and hence higher the cashflow. Through business process re-engineering you increase the net liquidity and reduce the net liability for a double-edged increase in your business cashflow.

How many business processes in your small business can you now get to re-engineer in the next 3-4 weeks that would meet the core objectives of this book? Ah ! It's all coming together now for you.

RE-ENGINEERING YOUR BUSINESS PROCESSES

I promised to take you through a simple business process re-engineering exercise without going through an elaborate Lean / Six Sigma process. So here goes – play along with me and follow these steps:

1. Pick any **end-to-end process** in your business. Start with just one, understand how this works and repeat for all of your other end-to-end business processes.
2. Open up a spreadsheet as indicated in Figure 9 and review the columns. Name this spreadsheet (**Current State**). Ensure you have a formula set for the Profitability column (Value – Cost). If you have a process flow diagram, great, if not, it may be worthwhile to simply draw up a process flow chart similar to Figure 7 for better visualization.

3. Start completing the data in each of the rows in the same sequence in which the activities occur in the process. If you don't have the data for the Cost and Value column when you get started that's ok. Move on to create the complete list of activities in the process.

ACTIVITY #	ACTION	ACTOR	DURATION	TOOLS & EQUIPMENT	MATERIALS & COMPONENTS	SUPPLIER ACTIVITY	CONSUMER ACTIVITY	COST	VALUE	PROFITABILITY	ADJUDICATION

FIGURE 9

4. If you were not able to complete the Cost and Value columns in Step 3, you will need to take care of this now for each activity. This would require some time for you to come up with these numbers as accurately as possible. Get organized and fill the values in those columns. You are unable to progress further without these two pieces of data completed for every row that you have listed in Figure 9.
5. With the cost and value numbers available, the profitability number should automatically be calculated for each of these activities. It should be quite interesting to review the sheet at this time. I am sure eyebrows will be raised as you review.
6. Copy this entire sheet into a new sheet in the workbook and name this spreadsheet **Re-Engineering**. Then sort the entire copied sheet in descending order of profitability. This will potentially disrupt the sequence of the activity list - that's ok.
7. Then evaluate a minimum of 10 least profitable activities – these should be at the bottom of the list. You need to make a

call on these activities in the "Adjudication" column.

8. In the Adjudication column for these least 10 profitable activities, specify one of the following
    a. Unchanged (no further action is necessary – it is what it is and absolutely no further improvement is needed)
    b. Merge (specify another activity in the list with which the activity can be merged)
    c. Remove (removed from the activity list completely)
    d. Automate (keep the activity but get it automated)
    e. Enhance (keep the activity but things need to be moved around for this activity to be more profitable)
    f. Reallocate (activity needs to be allocated to another actor with different skillsets)
    g. Outsource (keep the activity but it makes more sense to outsource it to a third party)
9. Now focus on the next batch of 10 lesser profitable activities in the list. Can you make any of them more profitable? If yes, follow the same adjudication process as in Step #8.
10. Repeat this process of Step #8 and #9, until you have covered all the activities in the list until every activity has something in the Adjudication column.
11. Copy this spreadsheet into a third spreadsheet and label it **"Future State"**.
12. Delete all rows that you have adjudicated as "Remove" – you have chosen to eliminate these activities in "Re-engineering".
13. Sort the entire spreadsheet in ascending order by the Activity # column and the rows will be sequenced in order.
14. Renumber the activity numbers so that you have a continuous sequence. Now draw out your Future State process flow with the new sequence of activities. You have just developed your version of an optimized Figure 8.
15. Implement the new business process flow in your organization and make sure you are measuring and monitoring the metrics.

16. Rinse and repeat this process every year, making the end-to-end process increasingly more efficient.

Every year meet with your Executive Leadership team and go through this process of activity optimization focusing your business on increasingly higher value producing activities. Your objective at each iteration would be to eliminate waste, increasing value and reducing cost of each activity, thereby increasing process throughput. Consequently your cashflow will continue to increase and you will be grinning all the way to the bank.

8 MODERN DAY LETHAL KILLER – CYBERCRIME
DON'T RISK YOUR BUSINESS TO BE COLLATERAL DAMAGE

In the new age of a technology-dependent world population and widespread Internet connectivity we have a new threat to the corporate world – Cybercrime. Cyberattacks can be launched literally at will on any company, anytime, from literally anywhere in the world over the Internet and yet the attackers can remain undetected and untraceable.

Some small business owners make uninformed assumptions that they are too small to attract any attention of a cybercriminal. Wrong! It could be a very costly mistake to make because these small business owners are not aware of the Mindset of a cybercriminal.

Cybercriminals do not care who you are, whether you are big or small. They are not necessarily after you as the direct target. However, in the event of a breach, your business and you personally as the business owner could take a direct hit. Cybercriminals are after the data that you store in your systems. More specifically they are looking for private information such as Personally Identifiable Information (PII) and Non-Public Information (NPI) for your clients and customers that you are hosting in your corporate databases or file system. If you are in the healthcare business, cyberattacks are carried out to steal Patient Health

Information (PHI) of your patients. Once data is stolen, the hacker has tremendous leverage over you and your business. By law and International Treaties, you are required and held accountable by regulations to protect the privacy and confidentiality of such PII, NPI and PHI data.

With such sensitive data breached and with copies thereof in possession of the hacker, they could sell that data to other predatory and criminal organizations who would use that data for unlawful purposes. If such confidential data has been compromised can you imagine what havoc it can cause to your small business?

Public embarrassment, negative media coverage, regulatory fines, lawsuits from customers, employees or suppliers who's data might have been compromised, even imprisonment, virally spreading social media rants are common. Not to mention huge customer attrition, loss of revenue, drop in product sales, increase of customer grievances, penalties, levies, investigations and destruction of the corporate image that you had worked so hard over the years to create. Bankruptcies and complete business shutdown are not uncommon.

As a small business owner, in this new age of sophisticated corporate espionage and cybercrime, you need to take every possible measure to protect yourself from such an attack. I have spoken to small business owners who use free public email systems and free public cloud systems to store sensitive data. *"We are too small to get hacked"*, they say.

One of my small business clients were hosting their operations with a reputed public cloud service provider who have billions and billions of dollars invested to provide such services. This small business got hacked on a Saturday night where the hacker got into the super user account of the server using a computer program (spambot) that logged in and out of the super user account 20,000 times in a space of 5 hours. The server logs did not show any indication at first for the client to know what all the hacker did while they were there. It wasn't until one of their system users reported an undocumented problem while using one of their web-based applications that a red alert was raised. Further research revealed that the hacker had actually penetrated into the application's source code and inserted a script that would steal the user name and passwords of any user who logged in.

This was a small business but generating a lot of interest in the market with their unique products and services. Never did they anticipate that they could get hacked and they did. You don't want to be in their shoes. Let's understand a little more about Cybercrime and Cybersecurity so that you are aware how serious this threat is to modern day businesses. I will then suggest some due diligence steps to follow to protect yourself from such cyberattacks.

MODUS OPERANDI OF A CYBERCRIMINAL

Who really is a "**hacker**"? Technically speaking a hacker is a person with a brilliant technical mind. They are thoroughly and intimately familiar with computer technology, networks and security systems. However they have "potentially" devious intent to cause harm and damage to life and property through unauthorized access to computer systems to manipulate or steal data, and/or corrupt internal functions of a software application or system.

Not all "hackers" are a threat to your business. We have the "white hats" who are actually penetration testers. You can even hire them for your business to give your cyber-defenses a workout to determine if they would hold up against an actual credible threat.

Then we have the "brown hats" who are 'benign hackers' - they don't attack to cause you any damage other than inflate their own ego to have successfully penetrated your defenses. Often times these are college kids who take a sense of pride to have hacked into your system and even playfully send you proof of their hacking event. You could use this as a warning system and take appropriate steps to improve your defenses in the event of a real attack.

Beware of the **"Black Hats"** as these individuals are not only brilliant and experts on the latest advances of computer networks, programming and operating systems, they are also researchers on how to beat your security defenses. They gain access to your servers with the intent to cause material harm and disruption to your systems and business operations.

These individuals have obsessive-compulsive personalities who have chosen to use their skills and knowledge for unethical and unlawful purposes. Black Hats would penetrate into the seemingly secure system, bypass security controls and spend most of their time stealing or altering confidential records in the file system or database.

The next level of Black Hats in the degree of notoriety and threat is the **Cyber-Terrorist** or the **Cyber-Criminal** who possess the expert skills. At times they even have access to insider connections in your organization to penetrate through the toughest security systems to cause deliberate harm and adversity to your business.

Some of these attacks can also place the general public in harms way. Such intrusions are not limited only to the theft or corruption of sensitive data. The cyber-terrorists may assume control of computer systems for public safety or even national security leading to mass inconvenience and disruption to public life and property.

As a small business owner, the Black Hats and the Cyber-Criminals are probably going to be your most formidable adversaries in this new age of the Internet Of Things.

HOLES IN YOUR CYBERSECURITY SHIELD

Now that you understand the threat let's talk about some of the most common areas in your small business that may be exploited by Black Hats and cyber-terrorists so that you become aware of where to strengthen your defenses.

VIRUSES, TROJANS AND MALWARE : Due to the worldwide popularity of Windows based systems and the sheer number of them connected to the internet, Windows based viruses, Trojan horses and malware have been the primary platform of choice for fledgling hackers.

BROWSER COOKIES : Depending on your browser security settings, cookies can be implanted on your corporate computers, smartphones and tablets used to visit rogue websites that monitor your browsing history, financial data, username and passwords etc. Once installed on your device, the malware can secretly transmit such sensitive information to a hacker's server leading to identity theft, abuse or even blackmail, ransom and extortion.

PHISHING : One click on an innocuous link in an email sent to a corporate email address, or unknown website could be game over for your business. Clicking on such a link could lead you or your unsuspecting employee into the execution of a series of scripts and algorithms that can expose details about the victims' computer and other secure accounts that they might be already logged into.

SNIFFING FROM FAKE WIRELESS ACCESS POINTS : When you use your corporate IT issued device to connect to free wireless networks in public places, you are exposing your device to hackers. They could *sniff* the network and gain access to confidential information stored in your device that is being transmitted through the wireless connection.

WEBSITE CONTACT FORMS / LOGIN INTERFACES : The most commonly overlooked and easily compromised areas of a website that could grant access to your internal systems are exposed email addresses and unprotected contact forms on websites. Poorly designed contact forms and application logins can be vulnerable to intrusion attempts such as SQL Injections and Cross Site Scripting (XSS), giving the hacker avenues to steal digital data from databases and also create data and database corruption.

PERSONNEL CODE OF CONDUCT : Unbelievable but true, 86% of intrusions in the last 5 years could be tracked down to employee and contractor misconduct and lack of due diligence when it comes to following prescribed policies and procedures for securely accessing systems where they are authorized.

CYBERDILIGENCE ON CYBERVIGILANCE

As a small business owner having a strategy and plan for instituting and enforcing cyber-security in your organization is vitally important.

Here are the **TOP 10** cyber-diligence practices that I recommend you understand and implement as soon as possible if you haven't already, to institutionalize the concept of cyber-vigilance in your business and strengthen your cyber-defense profile.

Screen your personnel and their activity – The most sophisticated security systems in the world can collapse like a deck of cards if an internal employee or contractor becomes the weak link in the defense.

So I recommend that you perform background checks of all employees and contractor personnel prior to hiring them and granting them access to your systems. User activity in your systems and applications should be tracked and monitored. Algorithms must be in place to raise alerts when unusual activity is detected.

Update and distribute Employee Handbook with your Cybervigilence and Cybersecurity policies and procedures – Transparency of the stringent controls you have in place for your cyber-security profile and employee conduct is important. They must be regularly communicated to your internal staff along with consequences of non-compliance. It is also important that you openly and regularly communicate the different ways an intrusion can occur.

Only corporate IT issued devices should be allowed to access internal corporate systems – this is very important for you to enforce across the board and all applications and networks must be configured to allow only approved devices to access internal systems. IT should be able to push updates to all connected devices. Remote connections outside the internal LAN must be made over a VPN connection.

Stay away from free Wi-Fi connections in public places – Employees should be prohibited from connecting their corporate IT issued devices to free public Wi-Fi connections in coffee shops, malls, airports, hotels and so on without a VPN. Consider signing up for secure Wi-Fi services such as iPass® for your organization, especially if you have staff who travel in the field as part of their job profile. If this sounds expensive, consider the use of 4G hotspots for remote access to the Internet.

Updated virus and malware signatures, SPAM filters - Ensure that all devices, to the extent possible, is set to automatically receive and install the most up-to-date antivirus and antimalware signatures to prevent contamination to your devices.

Update all security patches right away – Any sort of procrastination in installing the latest security patches to your firewalls, operating systems and applications could keep your infrastructure exposed to intrusions. Ensure that you update the security patches right away.

Keep extranet and intranet separate – Surprisingly enough this is often overlooked by organizations but is absolutely critical to ensure security of your systems. Your computer systems can be classified into three categories, which must be kept in separate networks. (1) those that serve the general public, which typically is your website (2) those that support internal operations (3) those that are used for electronic communication between business partners from other trusted organizations.

Secure your website forms and web apps – Ensure that contact forms in your website are set up to prevent robot or spambot exploits. If your contact form or web apps update internal databases in your webserver, ensure that necessary protection is in place to prevent SQL injections and Cross Site Scripting.

Consider hiring a Cybersecurity specialist – Major corporations have now opened up a new Executive Management position – CSO (Chief Security Officer). This position manages a team of Cybersecurity professionals who is tasked with one objective – protecting the company against cyber-attacks. If you are not in a position to hire an entire army of cyber-defenders, consider hiring consultants for a limited period to set up your defenses. Implement the necessary technology and procedures to detect, contain and neutralize cyber-attacks.

Alternative and Augmented Authorization – In order to improve the security of your internal systems and also for web applications that support logins, consider using additional augmented authentication modes like 3 or 4 Factor Authentication in addition to the commonly used username and password elements in the login process.

Get Sensitive Data Off The Public Cloud Or Shared Servers – While using public cloud platforms to store, exchange, and manage confidential data you are operating at a very high risk of intrusions, data theft and data loss. Read their terms and conditions of service and you will find that they are absolving themselves of any responsibility in the event that your data gets compromised. Consider web applications that can be installed on your own private server inside your intranet or use a private cloud for storing, exchanging and managing files and data containing sensitive information.

The temptation and enticement of low operating expenses to maintain your data in public cloud based systems can boomerang back very hard in the event of a breach. When the cloud is breached, the attacker is not cherry picking the data. They need to get in, do their stuff and get out as soon as possible after covering their tracks. They will attack to grab everything they can get hold of. If you are part of that stash, you become collateral damage.

Since you are reading this book and you appear to be serious about the core objectives here, it is evident that you are serious about your business and keen to take it to higher places. Cybercrime is a credible threat today and will seldom come to you with prior warning. When it comes it can decimate your cashflow, destroy your reputation in the market and potentially run your business to the ground. My intention is not to instill fear in your mind but in this case your Amygdala is doing its job well. So I appeal to your Cerebral Cortex that you need to adopt countermeasures against cybercrime sooner than later.

9 YOUR BRAND REPUTATION IS YOUR BOND
PROTECTION OF YOUR BRAND IMAGE IS YOUR TOPMOST PRORITY

My father used to remind me every now and then when I was a kid, "*Son, Your word is your bond. Choose them carefully and honor it with your life.*" That stayed with me all along and in today's new age of business regardless of size, that would read as "*Your Brand Reputation Is Your Bond. Protect It With All You've Got*".

Social Media channels, reputation management sites, blogs, review sites and websites are all open for everyone to share their opinions and views about your small business. Nothing gets swept under the carpet, especially trash talk. Unfortunately enough people today seem to gravitate more on the negative than on the positive. 1 less star in a review site like Yelp could imply as much as a 10% drop in sales. One negative comment out of 100 good ones can change the purchase decision of a lead that you might have managed to get into your marketing funnel.

Over 85% of consumers are searching for online reviews, social media posts and other online assets through search engines before making a purchase decision. Price, availability and feature lists are no longer the only criteria to make purchase decisions, your online reputation is also being factored in by the consumer before their Amygdala would allow their Cerebral Cortex to pull that credit card out. Every consumer is on a heightened state of alertness and they are looking for the greatest bang for their buck in a fiercely competitive market.

Negative reviews that are not addressed may lead to customer attrition and dry up sales funnels. In some cases the disgruntled consumer may even proceed with a compliant to the business bureau, file a small claims lawsuit or even provide content for nasty media coverage. Businesses who prefer to react than respond to such negative feedback have to spend tens or even hundreds of thousands of dollars on Public Relations Repair firms to do damage control in an effort to salvage the brand. As you can understand, negative points on your reputation has a snowball effect to seriously damage your corporate image and cuts your net cashflow with a double-edged sword.

On the flip side, if your business is attracting positive reviews where your patrons are literally singing your praises online, you are closer to don the crown of the king of the hill in your niche. Increased demand for your products and services, phones ringing off the hook, opt-in forms flooding your inbox, reporters knocking on your doors for interviews, are all possible when you are rocking the review sites, social media and other online channels.

Word of mouth even today, is the most powerful marketing strategy possible anywhere in the world. Online channels have made it easy, ubiquitous and instant to spread the word of mouth virally with high impact to modern day businesses. While it could be the golden ticket to prosperity, it could also be the most unforgiving obstacle in the growth path of your business.

What you need is a well-defined proactive Reputation Management and Implementation strategy that addresses online comments promptly and professionally. Positive comments and reviews need to be responded online with appreciation and gratitude. Negative comments and reviews need to be responded with earnest willingness to work with the unhappy customer and resolve the matter.

I want to refer you back to Figure 5 where I described how the human brain is wired – specifically how the Amygdala reacts and how the Cerebral Cortex responds. Your job as a small business owner in Reputation Management is to understand how both these reactions and responses should be addressed using the right choice of words that pacify an agitated Amygdala and appeases the euphoric cerebral cortex of your customers.

Here are some of the strategies you must implement in the online presence of your small business. These are the basics of what a PR firm would do for big bucks. Depending on the severity of the situation, you may just need to hire one for your business. But if the infringement is minor, you may be able to handle it yourself (and save a ton of money for your cashflow) by following these instructions. Just having an ordinary website is not good enough – you need to interact with your customers in the same channels where they are talking about you.

1. **RESEARCH** your exposure online and record everything by taking screenshots of every instance of evidence that you find – good, bad or ugly.
    a. Go to **PissedConsumer.com** (what a telltale name for a website) and search their database with the name of your company, your brand or any products or service that you have sold in the past. Record anything that you find in the search results.
    b. Go to **RipoffReport.com** (another suggestive name for a website). Repeat the same process and record anything that you find about your business.

c. Go to **bbb.org** (the Better Business Bureau website in the United States. If you are in a different country search website of a similar organization) and repeat the same process to record your exposure.
d. Go to Facebook, Twitter, Google Plus, LinkedIn, YouTube, Pinterest, Instagram and Flickr. Search for any posts made about your business. Search with your company name, brand name, product or service name with an without the "#" tag in front. Then follow it up with the "@" tag in front. Record everything you find.
e. Now open up Google and perform the same search with and without the "#" and the "@" tag. Prepare for a whole bunch of hits to show up (hopefully all the good). Bite the bullet, buckle up and go through each and every link that you find relevant. Record everything as you go along.

2. **ANALYZE** the results of what you recorded.
    a. Make hardcopies of every evidence that you found.
    b. If you are comfortable managing this using digital copies on your computer, make three folders and call them
        i. **Good (4+ star rating)**
        ii. **Bad (2- star rating)**
        iii. **Ugly (2.5-3.5 star rating)** (yes seriously – make it fun because some of the bad and ugly comments may be difficult to digest with a straight face)
    c. Copy each screenshot into one of these three folders as appropriate.

3. **STRATEGIZE** how you will address each piece of evidence on each of these categories. If you have access to a copywriter or a marketing person who is good at copywriting, have them write these out for you. Alternatively check or *fiverr.com* and you will get a ton of people eager to write compelling copy for you.

Every post you make, must directly address the person you are responding to by starting the sentence with "@nameOfPerson"

a. **Good** – prepare a post that expresses your gratitude for their kind words and your eagerness to serve them whenever they need support. A little bit of professional sweet talk never hurts. Put a smiley emoticon to end. Keep this to under 100 characters.

b. **Bad** – prepare a post that first of all thanks them for doing business with you and their candor to express their feelings openly. Follow up by expressing your empathy for their experience and if it is not too much against your grain, apologize for the poor experience. Remember that your business and its reputation are far greater than personal egos. You must use language to pacify their agitated Amygdala. Imagine yourself in their shoes – how you would expect someone to speak to you to calm you down if you were as agitated? Remain natural – feel their emotions and write a post offering whatever corrective action is appropriate. Full or partial refund, free replacement, another shipment, coupon for future order, prepaid debit card – take your pick. Put an apologetic emoticon to end. Keep it to about 250 characters max. You would need to shorten to 140 characters for Twitter.

c. **Ugly** – prepare a post to thank them for their business and their candor. Let them know that you have taken their comments as positive criticism and have taken measures to ensure that the problem does not recur in the future. Offer them a timed promotion on their next purchase and request them to post their candid feedback when they have a better experience with you in the future. Put a smiley emoticon to end. Keep this to 140 characters.

4. **RESPOND EXTENSIVELY** on every online channel that had the evidence of some comment about your business. Post the same or slightly modified content that you wrote up in step #3 in all of these channels as a Reply to the appropriate comments. If you have the email address and phone number of your "Bad" category customers, reach out to them with a personalized email with the same or slight modified content. If you are speaking to the customer on the phone, LISTEN more and remain patient about their grievances and do the best you can to remedy the situation. If your customer support staff are trained on NLP (Neuro Linguistic Programming) it is a bonus.

For sure there are impossible customers and trolls who would never be happy with anything you do. It is not worth your time and resources on someone who refuses to see reason. Record every interaction you have done with them – they may come handy if there is a lawsuit or FTC (Federal Trade Commission) compliant in the horizon.

It is not uncommon for strategic partners, suppliers, journalists and even potential employees to research the Internet as I have described here, before they make any commitments to enter and contribute to your ecosystem. Nobody wants to play with a tarnished partner.

Reputation management is not only to address a difficult customer but also to address your entire ecosystem and appeal to their confidence by getting past their natural Amygdala reactions and into their analytical cortical brain. As a small business owner, **proactive prevention** is a far superior and pragmatic strategy than a reactive cure in all areas of your business. With limited access to resources and the objective of intense and fast growth of your cashflow, you don't have the luxury to have your hard earned reputation tarnished by even one review.

10 BUSINESS LEVERAGE IN THE NEW AGE
CHANGING TIMES OFFER GREAT OPPORTUNITIES FOR LEVERAGE

Every small business owner anywhere in the world, more than anyone, appreciates the importance and potency of leverage in business. Leverage has been practiced down the ages in life and in business and has evolved over the course of human history in this planet. However under the current turbulent socio-economic-political and market conditions, perils of unpredictability in business impose tremendous stress and fear in the minds of all aspiring small business owners, entrepreneurs and startups. Traditional means of leverage still work but they are getting more and more scarce to the average small business.

Having said that, there isn't a single river in this planet that flows straight to the ocean from its source. It meanders around obstacles, finds a path all right to find the vastness of the ocean. We creative small business owners personify that river in real life and find our way through the toughest challenges, using tools and techniques available in these modern times. We don't just think out-of-the-box – for us, there is no box – just open doors of opportunities.

Did that resonate with you? Good. Let's discuss some new age leverage models that few small business owners are aware of. Opportunities are plentiful out there – be that river that meanders around rocks.

INVOICE FACTORING

Have you considered Invoice Factoring in your business to increase your liquidity, reduce your liability and hence increase the cashflow in your business? You may not have even heard about it and that's ok. Well, let's transition you quickly from your current state of unconscious incompetence to unconscious competence on this very potent leverage option for the new age small business.

Invoice Factoring is an excellent option to seriously consider to reduce the liability of deferred receivables from your customers in exchange of a small fee. While you can use Invoice Factoring for all of your receivables, it is probably more worthwhile to leverage this option for higher ticket sales that you have made under a deferred payment term contract. Here's an example of a real life business scenario when Invoice Factoring can come in handy.

Let's say that you have made a high-ticket sale for $10,000 with a client and have agreed to offer them a 30-day payment term. This is not a 30-day money back guarantee or a trial period situation, but a straight sale. They get to enjoy your product or service for 30 days before they would compensate you. Essentially your liquidity is stuck for 30 days due to this **Unsettled Cash** and hence your cashflow is stuck for the month. I have discussed earlier in Chapter 2 how you can structure your payment terms to incentivize your customer with tiered discounts so they make an earlier payment. Nonetheless, the customer may want to maximize their full payment term before clearing their payable. This is where Invoice Factoring can be your friend.

You find a third party company (referred to as the "**Factor**") who would purchase that open $10,000 receivable from you and make an outright payment of let's say $8,000 in exchange of that $10,000 receivable right away. Your Unsettled Cash just got settled for $8,000 within a few days of recording that receivable instead of waiting out the entire 30-day period. You still have $2,000 as Unsettled Cash – better than $10K, right? At the end of the 30-day period of the term, the customer enjoys their full term and pays the $10K directly to the Factor, because they now own the receivable. The Factor would keep say $200 as their fees and forward the balance $1,800 to you. From an accounting perspective, you have settled that $10K open receivable with $9,800 and the balance $200 is placed in an expense account for a tax deduction. Not a bad deal at all, right?

It may even turn out better than that tiered discount that you would have offered to incentivize the client. How would this strategy affect your cashflow for the month? That was a rhetorical question. Some small business owners pinching for pennies would frown at that $200 in expenses. Well, it's a personal choice and a business decision to make.

Will this work for every open receivable? Nope. Your Factor will perform their own due diligence before they agree to purchase your receivable. It is an investment they are making and every investment has its risks. So they will make every effort to mitigate their risk to make absolutely sure that they can recover the money and get paid for it. The quality of your product or service that was sold, the creditworthiness of your customer, their payment patterns are all considered by the Factor before they agree to take the burden of your liability.

What can you do with this increased cashflow for the month?

Make a search engine query on "Invoice Factor" and you will find a ton of options to consider, depending on which country your business is located. Perform your own due diligence before choosing a factor to work with not only for a one-time deal but perhaps on an ongoing basis. There are choices and you must be comfortable about the Factor before you engage in a relationship with them. Here are some considerations to analyze before choosing a factor.

1. **REALIABILITY** : How long has the factor been in business? That's easy to find out. How many companies do they work with? How much of funds do they have access to? Have they defaulted or delayed on that second payment in the past? Review the process of searching for reputation related data for any company as I have explained in Chapter 9
2. **PROFESSIONALISM** : You have a direct relationship with your customer and that is a high value asset for your small business. While they don't mind paying your Factor, but they would not be very happy with you if your Factor turns out to be aggressive beyond reason in their collection efforts. Note that the relationship between the Factor and your client in the process is purely a debtor/creditor relationship, which is quite different that your relationship with the client. While you would be softer and more professionally polite in your own collections strategy to maintain a good relationship, the Factor may just play hardball with your client to get their money. In that case your customer would have a bad experience dealing with your Factor and choose never to do business with you again. So although you might have done a quick cashflow boost using Factoring, you might have failed to retain that customer for future business. That could be a bigger strategic loss than a one-time cashflow boost. Also your reputation is at stake and by now you know how important Reputation is to a small business.
3. **CONTRACTS** : If you would be using the Factor occasionally, make sure you are not signing up for a long term contract with penalties of cancellation imposed upon you. When the Factor senses desperation in you they may try to bind you into terms that are unfavorable to your best interests. Stay cool and sign up for exactly what you are comfortable with. It never hurts to consult a lawyer familiar with invoice factoring before you commit to anything.

4. **PENALTIES** : The Factor is assuming the risk of your business and expects to get compensated for taking the weight off your hands. If your customer is late in their payments, the Factor may penalize you with additional fees that eat into that second payment due to you. In our example in this Chapter you may end up receiving only a portion of that $1,800 or nothing at all, if the customer has been late beyond their payment terms. Stay alert for these fees in the contract.

5. **HONORING THE CONFIDENTIALITY AGREEMENT** : You would have signed a confidentiality agreement with your customer before you started doing business with them. Inserting a third party such as the Factor in the mix typically is not addressed in such agreements. Even if you don't have such an agreement in place, as a small business owner you may want to retain the relationship with your customer instead of handing the reins over to the Factor. Note that the customer will be paying a different payee – not you. The Factor would notify your customer about this event. Your customer has some internal administration tasks to perform to make that Payee change in their accounting system. I would recommend that you retain control of communications with your client and not relinquish that control to the Factor until the receivable is paid. Make sure your Factor agrees to this "non-notification-factoring" in the contract with you.

6. **ALL OR ONE** : You have to decide as a small business owner if you are going to factor out all of your receivables for a customer or just one every now and then. Your Factor may require you to agree to transfer the receivable of all future invoices and seek to get a copy of all past invoices including their payment history. Depending on your needs for cashflow, make sure you sign up for only what you need – stay away from upsells. Note that your Factor needs you as much as you need them. Without you, they don't have any play. They are not doing you a favor for free, you

are using them as a value added service. Hold your ground and make a prudent decision.

As you can imagine, Invoice Factoring can be a very prudent strategic tool in your bag of tricks in modern day business to leverage OPM (Other People's Money) for your small business. Whether you are looking for a consistent cashflow with short periods of unsettled cash or you are looking for sporadic booster shots in the arm on an as needed basis, Invoice Factoring is a viable new age financial resource to tap into.

EUPHORIC MARKETING

For a small business owner, one of the biggest challenges is access to enough financial resources for marketing your products and services. Advertising rates in print and television are outrageous, pay per click marketing done incorrectly will suck out your cashflow like an industrial vacuum cleaner before you can even figure out what hit you. All of these channels of marketing in my mind are "Hope And Pray Marketing" strategies.

Out of the tens of thousands of marketing messages from companies clamoring for attention of your customers, you've got to have a pretty loud "voice" to be heard over the crowd. You need to be first in the line in order to entice a customer to listen to your pitch. Is that possible? Of course — at a price that would grind hard against your grain. There are thousands self styled marketing gurus out there with some bookish or theoretical knowledge at best and nothing but smooth talk to offer you. As a small business owner it can be quite confusing to figure out where to invest your limited marketing budget to maximize your ROI.

I have discussed the potency of proactive Reputation Management for your small business in the previous Chapter. It is a prudent investment that you would want to make to protect your brand. Why not leverage that investment in Reputation Management for some really powerful social media based word of mouth marketing – for free ?

Allow me to introduce you to **EUPHORIC MARKETING.**

Now that I have got your undivided attention, let's break this down and understand how you can leverage Reputation Management and basic Customer Relationship Management to get some powerful marketing - for free. Our key tool here is *word of mouth* and I will describe how you can use word of mouth for viral marketing in the new age of business.

You would have invested a fair bit in marketing for customer acquisition and in making your sale. That customer is now to be considered an asset for your small business. If the customer is coming back and purchasing more products and services from you, that asset just turned into a goldmine. If that customer is now starting to post some good reviews in the online channels that I have discussed in the previous Chapter, that goldmine just transformed into a rough uncut diamond. Why not nurture and shape that diamond, so that you enjoy the benefits beyond the first sale? Remember that you are feeding the pleasure centers of the Cerebral Cortex past a pacified Amygdala. Don't mess it up. Here's a recommended process.

1. Ensure that you collect the name, email address, residence address and phone number of your customers at every sale.
2. Track all activity in a CRM (Customer Relationship Management) system such as Salesforce.com or Infusionsoft.com – two popular low cost CRM tools for small business. Want to go cheaper? Use Gmail if you have to with the "bananatag" plugin. It will allow you to track actions taken by the recipient in Step 4.
3. After every sale send them an automatic email from the CRM system with the following pieces of content in your corporate

branded email template:
  a. Gratitude statement about the exact product they purchased in the transaction.
  b. Re-statement of the highest USP of the product or service they purchased
  c. If possible, provide a link to a short "how to use" video. When this image is clicked they are taken to a page where you have the instructional video playing automatically in the browser.
  d. What their purchase means to you as a business owner
  e. How they can contact you for after sales support
  f. Your commitment to help them maximize their investment in your product or service
  g. An uplifting quote that makes them feel euphoric.
  h. As a gratitude gift, offer a coupon for future purchases
     i. The coupon may be used by them (direct)
     ii. Their friends and family (broaden the offer)
     iii. Their social media connections (*leverage ++*) – ensure that you have all the major social media channel icons right below that coupon image. You would hyperlink each of these social media sharing icons to a page where you are offering the coupon for download and use by anyone.
  i. Closing gratitude statement.
  j. Sign the email with your name and signature. Not anything generic like "Customer Service Department", not any other name of any other person. Your name and signature as the grateful business owner.
4. In your CRM system, track the email for
  a. opens,
  b. actions taken on the hyperlinks,
  c. any forwards made.
5. If the email was not opened, place a customer service call

following the same pattern as above. If you personally don't want to call the customer, require your Customer Care specialist to open the call with "*I am calling from the office of <Your name>, the owner of <your company> to express our heartfelt gratitude you for your recent purchase of _____.* "

6. Search the social media channels regularly with the coupon's hashtag to find how many customers are sharing your coupons. When you find any of these shares, post a comment from your business account in the platform, thanking the customer for sharing and express your gratitude for their business. This is an explosive from a customer's mindset perspective. It is nitrous from a social media perspective.

7. Set up your CRM auto-responder on monthly schedule for the entire duration of the warranty period of your product (if you have one) to inquire how the customer is enjoying their product or service. A national holiday or festival coming up? Make sure to customize the email for the occasion. The idea is to stay in touch with a customer beyond the sale, demonstrating your faith in your product or service and also offering to provide assistance throughout the warranty period. What you are doing is to offer a lifeline, so that your customer feels well supported and taken care of – pampered !

Your objective here is to leverage the euphoria of a satisfied customer shortly after the sale is made and make an offer with that coupon for future purchases. You are not upselling or cross-selling in that email. You are celebrating their purchase and leveraging the endorphins in their brain to share that coupon with literally anyone they have a connection with. Some customers will also make a little post about their great experience while sharing the coupon on social media channels – that's BIG for you.

So there you go, free unbiased and voluntary word of mouth marketing, with instant social proof that your product or service is worthy of purchase, spreading virally through social media. How much money did you spend on this? None. Nothing over what you have already spent to acquire that customer. How much could you make out of it when the social proof hits the social channels? Even if you get one extra sale and repeat the same process with the new customer, how valuable is that for your reputation and for your cashflow ?

Leverage your investment on Reputation Management, combine the intelligence with CRM, understand and maximize the power of social media by leveraging customer satisfaction. You would have opened up new doors of revenue for your business without any additional marketing investment.

11 EARLY RETIREMENT TO YOUR EGO – TODAY

WHAT'S MORE IMPORTANT – YOUR EGO OR RAPID PROSPERITY?

As small business owners we have a very keen sense of pride and most definitely a strong ego. I mean come on, we're the guys and gals who have chosen to live outside the box. We're the explorers who have the audacity to venture away from the well-trodden path of working for someone else. We're the creative geniuses, who despite all odds, regardless of the toughest of challenges, have the courage to hold steady as a palm tree in the face of raging storms and figure it out. Sure we fall, you can count on us to make mistakes, but we still find the strength to get up on our feet to fight another day and create the highest value for those we serve. Way to go, pro! Time for a fist pump?

A lot of startups and entrepreneurs start a business with the solopreneur-mentality in mind. "*I can take care of it. Sure, I can do that too. Yup, I got that. I am the owner, sales person, accountant, designer, developer, marketer, reputation manager, customer service specialist, thought leader, technician ... what did I forget?*" It is a boon to your business if you really have the skills to be that Swiss-army-knife. But that egoistic attitude can be a threat to your business, to your personal life, to your relationships and to your health. All of these contribute to a threat to your wealth and well being. You may be able to get a trickle of money come in to barely keep the lights on, but in the greater scheme of things, forget about scaling your business to bigger, higher and greater things.

This is not to say solopreneur-businesses don't succeed – several online businesses are successful one-person operations. They have very little overhead with automated systems and they do quite well within their domain of expertise and income expectations. But they are definitely not in the dime-a-dozen category of flourishing small businesses. Imagine a solopreneur doing everything we have talked about in this book so far, all by themselves. The material covered in this book by the way is just a small fraction of what is needed to run a viable business.

You need to gather a team of highly competent professionals who buy into your dream and are willing to invest their skillset and infuse their energy to contribute towards your growth. It is natural for relatively new small business owners, entrepreneurs and startups to take so much pride in their independence. But at the end of the day, we small business owners need to understand and appreciate leverage. We need to appreciate the value of intellectual capital of qualified experts and seasoned professionals who can be brought to bear in the business.

Fortune grade companies spend millions of dollars every year to seek, hire or contract with such talented individuals to boost the growth of their business. They recognize and acknowledge that they don't know it all. Their core competency is in their own products and services and certain aspects of the business, but not all there is to run a world-class operation. Personal ego and pride is less important than the state of the business, its growth and consequently, the numbers that reflect its cashflow metrics.

That is why Fortune grade companies contract with qualified experts who have the skills beyond their in-house Intellectual Capital. The objective is to learn and apply **leading practices** in their industry and in certain cases, cross industries so that they can develop a best of breed business. Access to such unbiased expertise is often regarded as a competitive advantage for such growth oriented companies striving for operational excellence.

You may have heard about "*best*" practices. But here I mention "*leading*" practices. What's the difference and why do I choose to use "leading" practices and not "best" practices? You see, anything that is "best" seems to imply the ultimate, the final, as if the buck stops there and there is nothing better beyond. This finality is a sophomoric pipedream in the fast moving and ever changing world of business dynamics. How many of the new age strategies that I have already covered in this book were even a factor of consideration five years ago? Business dynamics, regardless of size are intimately tied to socio-economic-political and competitive parameters, which are continually evolving, morphing in shape, form and function. What was "best" yesterday is replaced by something better tomorrow, so business practices are always evolving, becoming more efficient, more intelligent, more metric driven. Hence my preference to use the term "leading practices".

It is not practical or possible for companies focused on growth, revenue and cashflow generation to keep abreast of these ever changing leading practices. That is where these experts come in. These experts have the unique advantage of working with several clients, getting exposed to a multitude of business cases and use cases all the time. They are constantly analyzing, testing, implementing, refining, improving business processes, technology, strategies to make their clients become better, bigger and scale higher mountains. These experts are creating real, intrinsic value every day for their clients. Is there a cost to contract with these experts? Absolutely. But the rewards of ROI are in multiples.

As a small business owner, you are heavily involved in the day-to-day activities in your operations. It is humanly not feasible, if not impossible to be aware of all the other strategies and techniques that are generating benefits for other businesses right now. Even if you were to be aware, what good is that knowledge without being able to apply it?

PROFILING THE RIGHT EXTERNAL EXPERT(S)

Should you hire to employ or simply contract with such experts? This is subjective and there is no straight answer. At times it is not your choice as a small business owner, regardless of what you would prefer. Some of these experts would only engage as a contractor and be reluctant or even decline your attractive offer for formal employment. There are pros and cons on both options, so you need to weigh them carefully. What's more important? Your ego for having employed the hottest ticket in your industry or to have been able to leverage the expertise and experience of the most qualified contractor on a time-bound basis?

You must look for experts who have both sound business **and** technical backgrounds with verified hands-on industry experience in what works in the new age of business. Every efficient business today has a large dependency on technology and there is no technology if there is no viable business. You want to maximize the ROI of your investment in contracting with these experts, which is why this blend of business **and** technology in their profile is very important to consider.

You are not looking for a theoretician or historian, you are looking for a field-tested, battle-hardened, hands-on practitioner, who can add intrinsic value to your business in the shortest possible time. With the limited funds in your small business, you haven't the luxury for hit-and-trials while contracting such experts. Stay away from self-styled business coaches who don't have verifiable expertise on **both new age** business management and technology appropriate for your business.

Otherwise, you may be able to get only half of the value at full price. Experts who are primarily technical, may not understand your business and would try to make your business fit inside their prescribed technology. That is sophomoric and you would want to stay away from such experts. The reverse is also true. You may find an expert who is fantastic at business strategies but they have no exposure on how to integrate processes and people with technology.

Your business processes and the strategies come first. If processes are not optimized, then they need to be optimized first around your operational metrics, before suitable technology and appropriate skilled resources are chosen to support those re-engineered processes.

You are not looking for theoretical sweet-talkers who appease your ego. You are looking for doers who would not hesitate to tell you facts the way they exactly are, even if it is uncomfortable for you to accept. Thoroughbred experts live by the rule that they have one mouth and two ears and they would use them proportionately. Hence make sure that they are listening more to your requirements and challenges than delivering their opinions and suggestions spontaneously, at least in the beginning. You are not looking for experts with bookish or boilerplate template-driven knowledge. You are looking for experts who have practical experience on whatever they are prescribing and appropriate to your business. There is no law or hardline that says everything that works somewhere else would also work in your specific business.

Business coaching and business consulting are two quite different skills and not every small business owner understands the difference. A coach would suggest and guide you based on preset patterns and theories that might have worked elsewhere. A qualified expert or business consultant that I am referring to, is a doer with tangible field experience and will not shy away from rolling up their sleeves to work in the trenches with you as needed. They may even actually set up prototypes if needed, consult with you and your team to empower you with the leading practices to make your business increasingly efficient. Just like you would not approach a general practitioner to get a brain surgery done, you would not contract with a generalist theoretician to solve your small business challenges, would you?

Leverage the brains of these experts for mentorship. Learn the leading tricks and tools of the trade. Collaborate with them to generate more value for your business, but never allow them to institutionalize themselves in your business. Some of these experts may want to stay on and on in your business, billing you for their services beyond the point of diminishing returns for your business. Avoid getting into such long-term contracts.

My recommendation for you is to have specific objectives when you contract with such experts and agree on a time period of their engagement to meet those business objectives. Part of your engagement contract must be a set of clearly defined objectives and deliverables that you would expect from your expert – a Statement Of Work. Knowledge transfer to your staff must be underscored in that SOW. The expert must make you or your designated staff self-sufficient in the shortest time feasible instead of getting institutionalized in your business. Otherwise their fees will erode your cashflow without ROI.

The right experts are in demand and there aren't too many of them. The same demand-supply parameters in standard economics apply to these experts as well. There is a price to pay to hire these experts and you must be ready for that and compare your investment with the ROI. For example, if you are paying $10,000 to an expert who would help you generate 5 to 10 times that amount or more in a space of 6-12 months, that is an investment worthy of consideration.

CHOOSING THE RIGHT EXPERT

Truth be told, the right expert for your business is not easy to come by and you cannot just pick them off the street. You must perform due diligence in your search for the right expert to mitigate the inherent risks of hiring an external non-employee. Here are some of the steps that I can recommend for you as you embark on your journey to find your leading practices expert to solve your small business challenges.

1. Search Linked In and then Facebook - the most frequented haunts of these experts. You would want to search for experts with the following criteria:
   a. Geographic location – 100 miles of your town
   b. Industry – your industry and any other industries that may be relevant to yours
   c. Experience – at least 15+ active years, depending on your type of business
   d. Publications in the market
   e. A resume if they have one available.
2. Visit their website, if they have one, to understand their message and how they express their expertise.
3. WIIFY – What's In It For You? Are they talking all about themselves or are they talking about you as well?
4. Ask your strategic partners for recommendations on experts who they might have worked with and derived tangible benefits.
5. Read their blogs and publications they may have.
6. Create a shortlist of these experts, connect with them, interview them personally or over video sharing applications such as Skype, Facetime or Oovoo to understand their body language, demeanor, professionalism and expertise.
7. This is a very important strategic relationship for your small business. Go beyond a phone call or email before you choose to

hire their services.
8. Use your business acumen in the interview to determine:
    a. Can they really provide value to your business?
    b. What qualifies them to deliver such value?
    c. Can they empathize with your current challenges?
    d. Do they have both business and technical backgrounds?
    e. Are they analytical and collaborative (use more of their Cerebral Cortex) or are they instinctive and prescriptive (more of an Amygdala-dependent person)?
    f. Do they sound desperate and over-eager to win your contract or are they presenting objective commitment to add value to you?
    g. What was the longest contract they served?
        i. Why did it take that long?
        ii. Are they making excuses?
        iii. Are they blaming the client?
        iv. What could have been better?
        v. What was the primary challenge?
        vi. How did they solve it? You are not interested to know the name of the client. You are interested to learn about their problem solving capabilities more than anything else.
    h. What was the most complicated challenge they were presented?
        i. how did they resolve it?
        ii. In what time frame?
        iii. Who else was involved in the solution? Were they part of a team or was it their leadership that solved the problem?
9. Determine if they would prefer to be engaged on a fixed price, a milestone based or a time and materials based contract. Are they wiling to accept at least a 30-day payment term? What works best for you from a cashflow perspective? Remember

that you will not see any results of your investment for a while until your expert's recommendations are applied.
10. Do they have references? Can you call those references? At times, non-confidentiality agreements don't allow reference calls but it does not hurt to ask. Your expert may have been effective in one business, which is good reassurance for you. But that does not guarantee they would be as effective on your specific challenges as well.
11. Sign an NDA (Non-Disclosure Agreement) with them before you reveal any information about your business that is considered corporate confidential.
12. When you are ready to sign an engagement contract, make sure it is a time-boxed contract with specific deliverables and expectations outlined clearly in the contract.

Once you have the legalities out of the way and your expert is under contract, engage them deeply into your business. Share your challenges, your current metrics, your objectives and let them get to work for you.

Listen to their recommendations – you are paying them for that. Sometimes facts they find and the recommendations they make may be hard for you to swallow. If you have to change certain things to meet your objectives, so be it as long as it makes business sense. Remember that your business is more than personal egos - it's about bigger growth, higher cashflow and fast-tracked prosperity. If you want things to change in your business you must change things that have a direct impact in your business. That is how you take corrective action and leverage the expertise of your expert to grow your business.

12 PROACTIVE TAX PLANNING
TAX AVOIDANCE IS LEGAL BY THE CODE, EVASION IS NOT

I am not a tax attorney and neither am I a tax planner, so everything you read about in this Chapter must be vetted with your tax planner or advisor. Depending on where you live and work, some of these strategies may not even work for you. Tax planning is an ocean and not everyone understands the prevailing tax codes to determine and recommend strategies specifically for small businesses to save on taxes. Nonetheless, minimizing your tax exposure can significantly reduce your mandatory liabilities and increase your cashflow.

WHO DO YOU LISTEN TO : I am assuming here that by the time you are reading this book, you would have already formed your business and you have made your choice of your entity type while incorporating your business. The purpose of this Chapter is not to challenge your selection but to address some new age tax planning strategies that your CPA or accountant would probably not tell you. Not because they want to keep things close to their chest, but because they are not required by law or trade to know the latest gyrations of the tax code.

CPAs and accountants are historians of what has already happened to the financials of your business. They would ensure that you are accounting for your liabilities and assets according to the prevailing laws, which in turn affect your business taxes. They are not business planners and do not make any forecasts on the state of your business. They can only work on facts, on real transactions and make a good job of accounting for them.

As a small business owner, your intent is to structure your operations in a manner so that you can take every deduction possible according to the current tax code, and hence keep more cash in the business – legally.

You have your business insurance agent, you may also have a Financial Advisor who helps you with your investments, you may have a CPA or tax preparer who prepares your taxes. All of these individuals have different core competencies and are feeding you with their insights independently. They are leaving it to you to collate all the data and figure everything out. How much insurance do you need to cover for what risk? What investments are prudent to make? When to move in, when to pull out of the investment? How does all of that feed data to your CPA? In what frequency? Where is the source of that data? How do all of these help you maximize your tax deductions? What else could you have done or could do proactively to save on taxes? When is the right time to make the right business decision that will make you eligible to save on taxes? What are you leaving on the table for the government to grab from your small business? You thought running a viable business was easy!

The tax code of the Internal Revenue Service in the United States is over 70,000 pages long. Every time a new legislation is passed the code changes. If knowing the tax code is your business, then you don't have much choice, but to be aware of all the implications of the changes as it relates to your business. It is no mean task. Moreover, not all strategies in the tax code are advertised to the point of making it common knowledge. So unless your core competency or easy reading book on a lazy afternoon is the tax code, you may consider hiring an expert on the tax code to give you proactive advice on tax planning to increase your cashflow.

PROACTIVE TAX PLANNING : Tax planning, insurance and risk mitigation strategies, strategic investments, entity type selections seem to be independent decisions made by different individuals with different views of the overall situation. The truth of the matter is these different areas are not divorced from each other and all contribute to your tax liability and hence your business cashflow. This is where pro-active tax planning comes in.

Why am I stressing on the word "proactive"? It makes more sense for you to adopt the necessary tax planning and implementation steps today, before the end of your accounting year, so that you can take those deductions. For example, if your business offers a voluntary retirement plan and you are making employer-matching contributions to your employee's plans, you may want to make all of these contributions before the end of the accounting year. Only then can you declare them for a tax deduction according to section 404 of the Internal Revenue Code in the United States. If you make that contribution after December 31st, then you can claim that as a deduction for the next year, not the current one.

Furthermore, you might have been able to claim a deduction through some strategy when you were starting out as a business, but may not be able to continue to use that strategy as your business grows. Your new tax planning strategy may negate the previous or because of your adoption of the existing strategy, you could be prohibited from adopting the new unless some other changes are made to your business.

Some business owners have the notion that proactive tax planning, that shows less taxes are owed to the government can increase their audit risks. This is FEAR (False Emotions Appearing Real) and nothing else. Proactive tax planning is not about avoiding taxes. It's about following the tax code in much minute detail to take advantage of all the possible authorized deductions to reduce the tax liability. As long as you are filing the taxes properly and your CPA is made aware of the strategies that you have adopted to reduce your tax liability, there should not be any more reason to flag a tax audit. Note that tax avoidance is not illegal, tax evasion however is breaking the law.

RETIREMENT PLANS : If you have chosen the 401K plan for your business, what analysis did you make to offer that type of a retirement plan? There are cheaper plans available to manage with more flexible investment options for the participants that might have been more beneficial from your tax profile perspective. Going with the flow like other businesses on retirement plans may not be the right choice for your business from a tax planning perspective. 401K plans are better suited for small businesses of 150 employees or more, but not recommended for smaller businesses.

OP-EX OR CAP-EX : Capital expenses need to be amortized over a depreciation period, while operating expenses can be deducted right away as long as they are qualified expenses. For example, if you are planning on purchasing capital equipment – such as computers, other machines, tools, hardware or even high-ticket software, they would need to be amortized. This means that your depreciation deductions are not realized upfront, which in turn locks up your cashflow. Technology has been changing rapidly in the new age, so the latest greatest today becomes a relic by the end of the depreciation period. You are stuck with upgrades and updates, which are also additional costs and expenses eroding your cashflow.

As a small business owner, consider leasing your hardware and even software. For example, instead of purchasing computers and laptops for your staff as a capital asset, why not lease them from the manufacturer and account for the lease payment as operating expense? When the lease period ends, simply return the old equipment and get brand new products under a new lease.

As far as software is considered, why not research if the software applications you need for your business can be accessed from the cloud? That may eliminate the need to have your own IT department, avoid having to maintain the infrastructure and manage everything. Migrating to the cloud can bring significant benefits when done right. You have to ensure that your data would be secure in the cloud. Data security in the cloud is major challenge in the new age of cybercrime as I have discussed in Chapter 8. An equitable position is for you to access the software applications in the cloud, but the data gets stored in your internal servers or in a private cloud over which you have complete control. If the software application you need, does not offer this distributed data management option, you may consider custom development. The good news is that software vendors are becoming increasingly aware of this need and are developing solutions that dis-associate the data from the application.

As you can understand leasing your technology infrastructure can significantly minimize that hole in your bank account and can also give tax advantages for your business when these expenses can be treated as operating expense.

MEDICAL EXPENSES : This is yet another area where you would want to seek professional advice on how to leverage this expense as a tax deduction. In the United States, the introduction of Obamacare has changed a lot in this matter. Even then there are some provisions for you to take deductions from medical insurance premiums.

Rising healthcare costs and the implementation of Obamacare has made businesses regardless of size to re-think their medical benefit plans for employees. A lot of small businesses have opted out from the traditional co-pay based plans into high-deductible health plans. The employees are encouraged to set up a tax deductible Health Savings Account (HSA) and pay lower premiums to cover for the plan. As a result employers are paying less premiums for the group health insurance plans and the employees are able to save on taxes through their HSA. If you offer health benefits to your employees, consider adopting a HDHP/HSA plan in the next benefits election period. You may be able to reduce your expenses on medical premiums, yet be able to save on taxes. Both of these will help you reduce your liabilities and increase your cashflow.

While your employees will be paying for healthcare from their HSA savings until the deductible is reached, their out of pocket for healthcare would be higher. Especially if they were used to a $10-$20 copay in the past, paying the full cost of healthcare until a pretty steep deductible is met, can cause some complaints from your employees, especially if they need frequent medical assistance.

The playing field on this matter has been pretty much leveled at the time of writing this book, as more and more employers are opting for HDHPs for their employees. A better health insurance plan is rapidly losing its competitive advantage from employer to employer.

As a small business owner, proactive tax planning, insurance planning, investment planning should all be considered collectively and proactively so that you can maximize your tax deductions and legally get to keep more money in your bank.

NEXT STEPS

We have come to the end of this book and you have now learned quite a few highly potent strategies that can easily double your business cashflow in the next 6 months. Is it possible? Yes. Can you make it happen in your business? You are the most qualified person to answer that. I have provided you with all the information and now the ball is in your court to determine where you go from here with this knowledge. Knowledge is power only when it is applied for a noble cause.

A fair percentage of small business owners will skim over the pages of this book, seeing but not reading. They would put the book aside and move on, leaving opportunities on the table that could have been leveraged. Their Amygdala won the battle, while the Cerebral Cortex lay neglected and lonesome, leaving them comfortable in the most uncomfortable time of modern day small business.

A smaller percentage of small business owners will read this book page to page, feel excited about the possibilities and vow to take action. Then life and business will happen and that excitement will fade away over time, also leaving opportunities on the table. Their Cerebral Cortex got energized with the euphoria of possibilities at first but then the lethargic inertia of the Amygdala overpowered that high energy to revert the small business owner into homeostasis.

A even smaller percentage of small business owners will read this book, will realize the several opportunities that are available and start preparing a list of action steps right away. They would assign skill sets required to implement the steps and send out email notifications for a kick off meeting with the team. They are already committed for a ROI on the time invested to read this book.

It is my belief and hope that if you are reading this message, you are part of this minority group of small business owners who don't think twice to seize the right opportunity when it crosses your path in life. If that is correct, I applaud your mindset and your professionalism as I have a lot of regard and respect for action-takers and doers.

Small business owners, entrepreneurs and startups such as you are those who are moving the world of business today – the right and conscious way. I would personally like to continue providing value to your life and business if you are interested to take your knowledge to practice further beyond this book.

As my appreciation to you for reading this book and being part of that small percentage of action-oriented business owners, I am willing to carve out 45 minutes of my time to speak to you in person *at no cost or obligation to you*. All you have to do is go to this link on my website - **http://gogetterstrategies.setmore.com** and schedule your session directly with me. When you schedule this short session, I will personally call you and collaborate with you about your business. During this call, please come prepared with your questions and your challenges. Perhaps I can provide some pointers for you to consider on the way forward and implement some of the strategies described here.

Why am I offering you with this free and no-obligation strategy session with you? As one small business owner to another, it's all about building strategic connections, networking, adding value to each other, with the possibility that we may actually decide to work together one day. During these calls I answer as many questions as possible, they like what they hear, they see the value I provide and typically would inquire if I would work with them on more professional terms.

If I believe I can truly add value to them and I have the bandwidth to provide that value, we talk terms and if all systems are a 'go', we get a NDA signed with an engagement contract and I get to work. I don't sell, I don't push, and I don't pitch anything during these calls. The primary purpose of this call is clear in my mind as a conscious small business owner – add value to my clients and prospective clients. I believe I have touted this philosophy throughout this book – adding value.

I have something more for you as a parting gift. As a further token of appreciation for your purchase of this book, please navigate to this link **http://gogetterstrategies.com/cashflow-book-register.html** to register your purchase. When you do this, you will continue to receive updates from me by email as new dynamics popup in the world of new age business that affects your cashflow. As you know the business dynamics change fast and it becomes quite a challenge to keep up with everything that is going on. I will keep you informed of these changes when you register your purchase at the link above.

So there you go, I have provided you with the next steps. Take action – if you have to read this book again, do so. Gather your team, strategize, break things down, analyze, rely on the power of your Cerebral Cortex and come up with an effective strategy to implement. Should you need my assistance, I am ready for your questions during that complimentary breakthrough strategy session.

As parting words, I would say, the world of business is changing, rapidly as the socio-economic-political changes seem to sprout up more frequently than ever before. As small business owners, we need to be nimble, age is just a number. There are school kids out there who would put us veterans to shame with their energy, their creativity and panache for business. My wish and intent for you is that you shine and thrive in your life and business exactly as you had anticipated (or better) when you started on your journey in the first place.

Peace and happy journeys through the new age of business.

ABOUT THE AUTHOR

Joy Ghosh has dedicated 26 years of his career serving small business owners and Fortune grade companies in the areas of business process re-engineering, enterprise software consulting, development and implementation, web application development, Internet and social media marketing.

An electronics engineer by education, Mr. Ghosh finds his passion to analyze and solve modern day business problems through modern day methods, strategies and technologies. After serving clients across 4 continents, Mr. Ghosh decided to grow roots and founded his company Go Getter Strategies, LLC . His core objective in this company is to introduce and implement effective Fortune grade strategies and techniques, adapted and rightly scaled for small businesses.

Joy serves in the Board of two technology startup companies. He is a small business owner, entrepreneur, published bestselling author, and a certified hypnotherapist, a certified social media intelligence analyst. On the lighter side, he is a second degree black belt in Tang Soo Do and is training to be a certified instructor in this martial art.

His website is at http://www.gogetterstrategies.com

www.ingramcontent.com/pod-product-compliance
Lightning Source LLC
Chambersburg PA
CBHW070253190526
45169CB00001B/388